God Moves Mountains

Yes, It Was a Miracle!

By

Marlys Norris

This book is a work of non-fiction. Names and places have not been changed to protect the privacy of all individuals. The events and situations are true.

ISBN: 1-4107-0009-7 (e-book)
ISBN: 1-4107-0010-0 (Paperback)

Library of Congress Control Number: 2002096612

This book is printed on acid free paper.

Printed in the United States of America
Bloomington, IN

1stBooks - rev. 02/21/04

GRATEFUL ACKNOWLEDGEMENTS

IN LOVING APPRECIATION TO
THE ALMIGHTY AND MAGNIFICENT GOD OF THE IMPOSSIBLE,
WHO ULTIMATELY BROUGHT MY BROTHER
"HOME AT LAST"

To my sweetheart husband, Richard
for his loving support, encouragement, strength and courage.
The Lord used him as His willing vessel
Blessing my parents and me with the "Desire of my Heart".
To bring about a lifetime hope of reconciliation
Of our family.

To our beloved and loving parents
Mildred and Marvin J. Johnsen

To our loving daughter Linda

To the kindness of many strangers who passed our way

To our "Angel" Bill Meng
For his loving support, translating and devotion
as he helped us do good for others.

To Meg Donahey
for that very important phone call

Thanks to friends
for editing my manuscript.

DEDICATION

"TO THE MISSING/LOST AND/OR ABUSED CHILDREN EVERYWHERE"

GOD DOES LOVE YOU!!

SPECIAL DEDICATION TO

JOHN & REVE WALSH

FOR THEIR LOVING CONCERN FOR PARENTS OF MISSING AND EXPLOITED CHILDREN..

Children are God's gift to mankind, entrusted to raise with love and security. Children give families a sense of longevity. Always protect and love them and they will love their own children.

AND

JAY SECULOW

THE AMERCIAN CENTER FOR LAW AND JUSTICE FOR HIS CONTINUOUS WORK TO SAVE OUR LIBERTIES, PRESERVE OUR PEACE AND FREEDOM FOR ALL OUR CHILDREN

TABLE OF CONTENTS

GRATEFUL ACKNOWLEDGEMENTS iii

DEDICATION v

Part I 1

The story begins with the summer vacation to a wealthy couples summer home on an island in Rainy lake between Minesota and Canada, A vacation that changed the structure of our family forever when the socialite woman takes my brother Craig to California instead of returning him home.

Part II 25

Mother cannot wait any longer and goes to California to bring Craig home. The surprise visit and confrontation with the woman and her outrageous threats and abuse to Mother. The chauffer has a gun.

Part III 45

Gilda arrives at our home and "kidnaps" Craig and goes to the island. Dad follows and brings him back. Parents forgive and forget when she appeals to them! This results in a second summer vacation at Red Crest Island for Craig and I. She repeats her past offense and does not return Craig to our home and finally the valet brings Craig home. Harassment follows and many celebrities and famous people come to the home.

Part IV 53

What kind of people would believe information from others without proof and facts relating to a child's terminal illness? Why as parents were their rights overlooked, hindered even by

the laws that is there to protect them? How could this happen to parents who loved their children?

Part V 71

Legal battle begins. Gilda takes Craig off to Florida and doesn't show up in court. Becomes too big a battle for our parents! No other choice but to let go and let God.

Part VI 81

My search is birthed again with the adoption of our daughter. New adoption papers filed for Craig. Mother goes there in hopes of seeing her son. He is doing research for Sam Houston Johnson's book, "L.B.J.".

Part VII 93

The Lord changes my heart and also my letters I write to Gilda. She responds.

Part VIII 99

Agape love birthed in me. We receive first photo of Craig in 15 years. Communication begins My reunion in Mexico with brother, after 27 years. Gilda dies leaving Craig destitute in Mexico

Part IX 115

Craig is paralyzed from cancer in Mexico. We go to his aid and God moves a mountain for us miraculously.

Part X 133

Everyone had passed away. Copies of legal affidavits enclosed as proof of the truth of this story.

Craig in 1939 – 41 - 42
Mother – Dad – Cousin Penny
in front of Grandparents homes in north Minneapolis

Easter Sunday 1944
Grandmother Hultgren
Marlys – Craig – Penny

Dad – Marlys – Mother
1936 or 1937

Mother – Dad
Craig – Marlys

Craig – Penny – Marlys
Grandfather Hultgren

Mildred and Marvin Johnsen
50th Wedding Anniversary

GOD MOVES MOUNTAINS

YES, IT WAS A MIRACLE !

By Marlys Norris

Little did we know the day had arrived that would change the structure of our family forever and the course of events that followed would cause all of us misery beyond our comprehension.

Mother – CRAIG – Dad
Last Visit Home interrupted by policeman at our door!

PART I

THE SUMMER VACATION THAT CHANGED OUR LIVES AND SEPARATED OUR FAMILY FOR THIRTY-SEVEN YEARS.

Little did any of us know, this vacation and association with very wealthy people would cause the greatest heartbreak and suffering of all our lives. Or that it would bring about a separation and constant "abuse" to our little family that cannot define description. It continued for years because the millionaire Dahlbergs, with their influence and unlimited finances were able to do just about anything they wanted and get away with it. The mental, physical and emotional abuse caused to my parents and myself was unbelievable, not to mention the irrefutable harm done to a darling little boy named Craig.

UNCLES ARRIVAL AND OUR TRIP TO "RED CREST ISLAND"

It was a hot July 23, 1944 day when Uncle Milton came home in a beautiful shiny yellow convertible to take us to an island near the Canadian border called Red Crest in the Lake of the Woods. The millionaires were going to spend the summer on their island in Rainy Lake between Minnesota and Canada. Uncle Milton drove one of their cars so they would have transportation to go shopping over the border while they were on main land.

He stopped in Minneapolis to visit his folks. He followed Aunt Louise, Grandmother and cousin Penny and came by to see us. Evidently he and Mother had talked prior to his arrival about the wealthy couple inviting my brother and me to their island for the summer. The millionaires told him all of his family was welcome to come up during the summer. They thought it would be especially nice for his niece Marlys age eight and nephew Craig age five to drive up in the car with him.. Mother had us dress in our Easter best and packed our clothes in a suitcase. Before we knew it we were on our way in the shiny yellow convertible with Uncle Milton, everyone waving goodbye.

While driving along, Uncle Milton sang lots of songs. He had a beautiful voice and it seemed to bring him a lot of pleasure singing along with the radio. Mrs. Dahlberg, (Mrs. Millionaire), had written grandmother that she heard it said that he and Mario Lanza had similar singing styles and sounded much alike. They had sung together in "Winged Victory" in New York a year or so before. This is when Mrs. Dahlberg had first met Mother and Dad, myself and Mother's younger sister Louise and (Gilda-Beth) Penny who was named after her. We had driven to Norfolk, Virginia to help her bring her things back to Minnesota when her husband was transferred overseas.

Years before, Uncle Milton had left home after high school to seek a singing career and he had landed a job in International Falls in a nightclub when he was seventeen years old. One night the Dahlbergs were there and heard him sing and motioned him over to their table during intermission. Mrs. Dahlberg was very impressed with his musical talent telling him what a wonderful voice he had and that she wanted him to come to their island and sing for her houseguests. She sent the boat over during the next day and while he was there she convinced him to go to California with them and she would help him further his career and he would become a famous singer. Intrigued, Uncle Milton agreed and all he really did was sing for his lodging and meals. Of course, he was introduced to hundreds of celebrities in Hollywood, Beverly Hills and New York as they were regular guests to parties held by the Dahlbergs. He easily became accustomed to the lifestyle and loved being around such interesting and creative people.

Dressed up for the trip to the Island

It was hot and humid and mother had us dressed in our Sunday best to make a good impression on the couple who had invited us to their island. Those days, we did not have air conditioning in cars. The wind helped cool us down as we drove along in the convertible. The trip was long but the breeze made it bearable. I thought it was really exciting to be with our uncle who was the "talk" of the family. It seemed like he was a celebrity of our family. It was exciting for everyone to hear him talk about all the movie stars he had met as part of the "Hollywood Scene."

The two-lane road seemed endless and straight as we drove along with huge trees on either side. The road did not seem to have many curves or turns in it but it certainly was beautiful. About four hours into the trip we stopped for some gas and a cold drink. I guess our uncle didn't think about us children getting hungry because he never offered to buy us anything to eat.

We arrived about eight hours later in International Falls. Our uncle had called prior to our leaving and they estimated how long it would take us to get there. A speedboat was waiting for us at the dock in International Falls. We got in and had a 45-minute ride to the large island called Red Crest also known as Swordfish Island on the maps. Approaching the island, we saw a huge Indian teepee, then a large house over a high cliff with a huge rock porch surrounding the exterior. We passed it and saw a couple smaller houses and small alcove and a dock they used for a swimming area. We arrived at a large boathouse with a loading dock alongside where we stopped and were told by the man driving, " It is time to get off the boat, we are here folks!"

It was a breathtaking sight with the green trees, blue sky and water. Our eyes must have been like saucers as we were ushered up a hill to the great big house. Immediately we were taken to a bathroom off a bedroom and told to wash our hands and faces and get cleaned up for dinner. I helped Craig and we washed our hands and faces. Then, we met in the dining room. Mr. and Mrs. Dahlberg and Uncle Milton were sitting at the table in the dining room and greeted us as we entered.

The couple welcomed us to the formal dinner table, set much like our grandmother's at Christmas. We were introduced and instructed to call them Bror and Gilda, not Mr. and Mrs. (*This was improper from what I understood about etiquette but that is what we called them.)* I could see that the millionaire lady hostess (Gilda) took immediately to my brother.

The first few days my brother and I were treated alike. The days that followed she would plan things with him leaving me to fend for myself. Gilda was childless and about fifteen years older than our mother. She had black hair and dark glaring eyes and was about five foot tall. She had a low raspy powerful voice and she dressed young for her age. She wore large earrings and big rings on her fingers. Her fingernails were painted in a bright red. She wore strong perfume. No matter what she wore in clothing, her tiny feet were endowed with shoes with bottoms that were about two inches high. Just like the shoes worn by Latin movie star Carman Miranda. Gilda had a harsh low tone to her voice and her dark glaring eyes scared me. I didn't mind not being around her or that she did not say much to me. I quickly observed that when she wanted me to answer favorably on something she would refer to me as "darling". And I did respond as she wanted, out of fear. Instinctively I knew the way I was "expected" to answer her. I wanted to stay on her good side!

The wealthy man (Bror) had a distinguished air about him as he sat at the end of the table. He had blue eyes, gray hair, a friendly face and a gentle voice. He was about the age of my grandfathers. Bror had a gentle look and spoke kindly to me and I really liked him. After dinner Gilda rushed Craig off to another room close to her.

The next day after lunch, Bror received a telephone call and shortly after left the island and he never returned. He had a thriving business and had to return to Chicago. I do not remember having meals with my brother after Bror left the Island. .

Craig and I previously had meals together, then, all of a sudden I was told to eat with the servants in their quarters and was not treated the same. Being the oldest, I used to watch over Craig a lot. I was getting used to Craig having more attention at first and it did not bother me, nor was I alarmed. She kept Craig rather secluded somewhere in the house and I hardly even saw him.

The next morning the air was fresh and brisk. I woke early and decided to take a walk among the pine trees to look around. From the big house I went the familiar path we had taken the day before, down the hill toward the boathouse. I hadn't gone very far and the bell rang. I had been instructed the previous day—"when the bell rang, it indicated no matter where I was, I was expected to wash and go in for a meal." I scurried up to the house and saw Gilda doting and fussing with my brother in the dining room. Craig had his own agenda when it came to eating. He never liked his food to touch and he would eat one thing at a time. He usually didn't have to be coaxed to eat but he would eat at his own pace. Now having to eat foods that were unfamiliar to us presented a new problem.

Craig was a very slight person, much like our Dad when he was the same age.. It was also the normal weight for people of our family. Dad's side of the family was slight build and mother's side was short. (*Later, you will see how Gilda made the weight an issue making a false case of "neglect" against our parents. Do the photos appear that either of us was neglected? Of course they had two other normal healthy children at home, but the no one ever checked or commented on that!)*

Gilda seemed overly concerned about Craig's eating habits and constantly coached him to eat more food. (*Yet as years progressed this never had any impact on his physical makeup because it was normal for him.)* She insisted that he eat the way she believed was correct. Before I was told to eat elsewhere, I could see that he was becoming more aggravated by her constant coaxing. I was very protective of my brother and I am sure that she sensed my sisterly concern for him. She would not allow me to say or do anything on his behalf. When I said anything at all—she would become very authoritative and obviously angry with me. Realizing Craig had no choice, he complied with whatever she said. Passive children most always respond favorably and Craig was a passive child.

Today, I know Gilda had a bigger plan in mind. She had "fallen in love" with this darling blond, blue-eyed boy child and wanted him as a possession, just like she had become infatuated with my uncle so many years before and convinced him to change his last name to Dahlberg. . She wanted a son of her own and unable to have a child she decided she would take Craig from this young family. As years passed she accomplished her goal in some ways but not completely because she never completely captured Craig's love for her as a real "mother!"

Separating us at meals and as much as possible was her way of keeping us apart with the hope that our attachment as brother and sister would diminish *forever. She was already attempting to have complete and total control of his life. Her sinister plan had already begun to take shape.*

On this so-called "fabulous vacation" I had to find things to do for myself. I was often left alone with no one to even talk to me. There were times when they would take Craig off the island to town and left me on the island with the servants. As I would watch the speedboat take off without me I felt tearful and not understanding why they had left me behind. Even as a small child of eight years old, I was a person who tried to accept and make the best out of any situation. A quality I saw exemplified often in my parent's lives.

When they left the island, I would entertain myself and relax around the huge round fireplace with a big bear rug and play very old records. I enjoyed singing and learning lyrics of the old songs I had never heard before. I thought it was fun because I could sing out loud to my hearts desire and pretend I was a big movie star. My grandparents had a record player too, and when I would stay at their home, I would wake before my grandparents. I would put on one of the records Uncle Milton had made and sing to my heart's desire. My grandparents didn't mind. I would sing with him and drink Dad's Root beer. I think my grandparents liked to see me do this because a few times I saw a funny grin on their faces.

FISHING!

One time I ventured into the boathouse and took out some fishing gear and went to the dry dock and proceeded to fish. I don't remember what I used for bait. I had some experience fishing with grandpa and grandma Johnsen on the Minnesota lakes and I knew I could catch a fish. I enjoyed fishing and thought it was so much fun.

I decided that I would fish in the area where we went swimming. The sun was bright and the sky was a radiant hue of blue. I launched my line as far out as I could throw it and waited what seemed like only a few seconds. All of a sudden I had a big bite on my hook, I pulled and pulled and pulled and finally pulled it in. It was the biggest fish I had ever caught in my whole life. No one was around and it was real heavy but I managed to carry it up to the house. I wanted to show it to everyone. When they saw my catch they told me it was a "Northern Pike". I was very happy and excited and I really enjoyed getting everyone's attention! Everyone was amazed and praised me for my efforts. I remember telling everyone how I had gone fishing with my grandparents and caught a big black fish, almost as big. Grandpa called it a catfish, but we had to throw it back in the lake because it wasn't a good fish for eating because it lived and ate on the bottom. The servants cooked the Northern Pike and we had it that next night for dinner! Poor old fish!!!

Eventually being by myself so much of the time did make me feel lonely for home, family and friends. I really began to miss our parents and grandparents. I was old enough to write cards to Mom and Dad and when we went to town, I mailed them.

One time I was asked to go to town, only to be told by Gilda, "Now you just walk the streets and entertain yourself!" (*Had my parents known I was left alone in a strange town, they would have been very upset with the way I was treated. They assumed I would be taken care of the way they did. They never asked and I never told them about the many incidents similar to this incident that happened to me.)* I did not know where everyone went and I just waited at the boat until they returned. It seemed like hours.

Afraid to venture very far away, I feared they would just forget me and take the boat back to the Island without me. I waited near the dock and time seemed like an eternity. They returned laughing and didn't seem concerned for me at all.

(*Both my brother and I were quiet and passive children. I may have been a little more expressive than he, but not very much. I had been taught a child "should be seen and not heard" and to be good!*

Our parents were never harsh or abusive in any way. As I have matured, I have been able to be a bit more expressive with my thoughts and ideas and to state my opinions.

THE NORTHERN LIGHTS OR AURORA BOREALIS

One night the sky was exceptionally blue as the sea and ever so clear. It seemed as though I could almost touch the stars in the sky they seemed so close. As I looked northward, I saw a stream of light, which formed a fiery arch of great beauty across the sky. Its rays were transient and constantly in motion, varying in color from blue and green to orange and pale yellow, to a deep blood red with its shapes infinite in number.

As I gazed upon this spectacular sight, I thought about ballerina dancers in their colorful costumes dancing around and around. The Aurora Borealis seemed to cover the whole sky and its rays made the night as bright as though sunshine was raining from the sky.

This was the most beautiful sight I have ever seen of nature in my life. As I stood in awe of its beauty I knew there was a God! . Even as a child I would look with wonder and amazement at the beauty in nature that God created for us to enjoy.

LONELY FOR FAMILY AND HOME

After a few weeks of this, I really began to miss home more and more and possibly even expressed my longing for my parents. I wrote home about it and shortly after I was taken by one of the servants to the Greyhound Bus and shipped home like I was some kind of package….all "alone". I didn't know why my brother was not returning with me.

I was only around eight years of age and had never traveled alone anywhere. I felt almost paralyzed with fear when I was told I had to change buses in Bemidji. However, an adult traveling on the bus told me to just wait and the bus would come along in short time.. I never questioned anything adults made me do but just did it, regardless of what was happening inside me. I was so shy.. The bus driver reassured me I was in the right place to catch the bus, but that did not relieve the anxiety inside of me. It was a long lonely trip home.

In Bemidji, I waited outside for the different bus. The bus stop was beside a park and I saw the big statue of Paul Bunyon. It was about 100 feet away and super tall.. I had never seen anything as big like it before. I was so afraid and the feelings of rejection, abandonment and desertion brought on by the person of Gilda who just coldly sent me home made me sad.

I had never experienced rejection before in all my life. This trip with all its natural beauty held many dark moments in my memories. I was so glad I was headed to where I wanted to be…home and all the security it represented to me!. Passive children just obey. I never asked anyone why brother Craig was not going home, I merely accepted the decisions of this adult. Soon after I got home, I felt the guilt for leaving him alone and it never left. I felt I had been selfish and blamed myself for leaving him. I assumed he would return with my Uncle Milton when he came back from the island, traveling to California in the shiny yellow convertible.

(*When I was a child while in the care of this woman I was subjected to several events that marked my own development. Having experienced fear, fear became my dreaded companion and I struggled to cope with it all of my life. As a child I passed through those times of tremendous inner turmoil. The sadness and anxiety they brought into my life have caused a condition called Agoraphobia. Although I am better today, it has been a lifetime struggle for deliverance. My scope of safety and security has enlarged, but the fear of an anxiety attack crippled my life.*)

BAD NEWS TRAVELED AHEAD OF ME

Traveling on the bus trip back to Minneapolis, my thoughts of why my brother was not sent with me were so puzzling. He was three years younger, very timid, passive and shy as well.

I arrived home safely only to learn that my brother was not returning until the following summer. Mother and Dad seemed exceptionally troubled and concerned. They related to me some tragic news and Gilda had just taken Craig directly to California without my parent's full consent. I overheard them talking about his dying if he stayed in the cold winter in Minnesota. They mentioned something about red and white corpuscles, (Leukemia) but I had no idea what that indicated. I just did not understand this at all. My brother seemed to be a healthy, normal, quiet, sensitive little boy to me. I heard something about these people taking him to a doctor in International Falls, and that was what the doctor had diagnosed.

Mother and Dad were very trusting and probably very naive. They were in their early thirties and Dad was a mailman with a modest income. My brother's health appeared to be a very serious problem. They were frightened when they heard their son would die and he needed to live in a warmer climate.

They had no reason to doubt that these people were telling them the truth. They were older, wiser and thought they were very knowledgeable and honest. Mom and Dad believed in the goodness of others, so it was only natural to believe this couple was sincere in every way, kind and good as well as anxious to help.

The Dahlbergs informed my parents that they would take Craig to the best doctors and nurse him back to health. They would send him to one of the best private schools in warm and sunny Southern California. Gilda would personally supervise his diet and he would be as "good as new" (*her exact words)* when Mom and Dad saw him again. Mother's brother Milton would be there, and surely he would advise my parents immediately if they were needed. The Dahlbergs were older, very well off financially and they assured Mother and Dad that it would not be a burden for them.

Mother and Dad deeply appreciated this couples' concern and kindness and the offer of medical help for Craig. Mother wanted to be with her son and reminded by Mrs. Dahlberg that she also had a daughter to care for. Her heart was torn in two. They didn't have enough money for her to travel back and forth from Minnesota to California.. She didn't know what to do. They were so shocked and very—very scared about the condition of their son. Without even seeing any "proof" of the doctor's reports they *just believed this couples every word.* I don't think they even asked for any evidence of this diagnosis. That's what my parents were like—trusting in the goodness of others all of their lives.

Ironically however, while they were talking about what they should do and considering "if they should let him go" with my uncle to California. Gilda did not wait for their answer and took off with him. (*Note: Did she fly out of the twin cities airport and never made an attempt to even s top by our home?)* When my parents found out, they were very upset, but certainly did not want their son to die. After many discussions—the Dahlberg's convinced them to let him stay in California until the following summer.

A year passed with constant contact with phone calls, letters and gifts were exchanged.

Summer came. and Craig did not come home. Many phone calls and letters followed sent by my parents requesting that their son be returned home. Mother was pregnant and they had too little money to go and get him. Learning the couple sent a invitation for all of us to go visit them in California after my sister was born in January 1945. Mother and Dad kept requesting his return and were helpless to go and get him themselves.

There was very little talk in our home about the whole incident as the excitement about the new baby's arrival. Finally on January 30th little Cheryl was born and everyone commented on how beautiful she was. Taking care of my little sister Cheryl, helped to fill the void in all our lives that we felt after Craig was taken. It is understandable why the Lord blessed our family with another child just at that time. Mother poured the love she could not give my brother into my baby sister as her presence helped fill the void in all our lives.

Something was still very wrong... Our family is separated ! !

Request after request were made to the Dahlbergs to return Craig to his home. Finally they agreed that he would go home in the Spring. Gilda continued to make one excuse after another. He was sick and the doctor did not want him to travel. He had plans with his friends. He shouldn't have his school year interrupted! You name it they said it! Then their request for my family to go to California and visit him instead arrived. The family was to come as their guest and they would pay for the train fares. Mother yearned to see her son and know that he was really all right so she agreed to go taking Cheryl and I along.

All of a sudden, Mother, sister Cheryl, and I were on our way to California. When we arrived I was registered in the same grammar school in Beverly Hills where Craig went. Mornings we would eat breakfast in the servant's quarters and be taken to school by the chauffeur.

However, Craig would get out earlier and the chauffer would pick him up. But when school was out, I was left alone to walk home up the hill about two miles to the top of Alpine Drive in Beverly Hills. (*How they figured I was smart enough to know the way back, when no-one took time to show me the way home, I will never know!.*) It was an exclusive part of the city and it certainly was a beautiful walk with gardens, flowers and beautiful homes. Many movie stars lived along the way and as I passed their homes I would look hard to see one of them. Some homes along Alpine Drive belonged to Lorraine

Day, Wallace Berry, Marie Dressler, Theda Bara, Lex Barker (First Tarzan), Walter Mathau, Phil Silvers, Mark Tapar and on Roxbury Drive, Rosemary Clooney.

The front of the Dahlberg estate was graced with a circular driveway and if you stood at just the right place you could see the swimming pool off to the left. It definitely was the rich part of town and nothing like where we lived in Minneapolis. Later I was told that famous people such as John Garfield, lived back of them on Cold Water Canyon.

Walking home from school, I was exhausted after the hike up the hill to the house and when I finally got to the house Mother would make sure there was some kind of snack for me because that was what she did everyday at home.

Again at dinner times I had to eat in the servant quarters just as I did at the lake. I had good manners and was accustomed to using crystal and I did not understand this treatment. I did not understand my mother not insisting that I eat with everyone. (*only in later years did I understand my mother's weakness and her fear of Gilda)* Being left out really hurt my feelings. This was a time when Gilda could degrade and intimidate my mother in front of my brother. She thought this made herself look like the loving, wonderful, strong and knowledgeable one… Her purpose was to hopefully make my brother think of her as mother and he would love her more. I was there when it happened, I objected to the treatment and Mother began cry. I came to her defense and Gilda did not like having anyone oppose her.. Obviously Gilda did not want that scene repeated in the presence of my brother. I would remember and also ultimately "tell" someone someday and she wanted to invalidate anything I said to anyone.!

(*Knowing my brother (later) I doubt he was ever able to feel any real love for Gilda as a Mother. She never let him develop into a complete human being. Instead, she manipulated his life and used him for her own purposes giving him little freedom to explore his own talents.*

He knew he had his own natural mother and he had certainly felt Mother's love as a small child many times. In a strange sense of the word that seems a bit sad after all the love Gilda believed she had for him during her lifetime and all she did to "possess" him as her son.)

I never asked why I had to eat in the kitchen area. Possibly she just did not like me. I didn't like her either. I never knew why I was treated so rudely. Sometimes Mother did make excuses to be with me or I would feed my sister so Mother could be with my brother. .

(*When I think back I wonder if I was some kind of threat to this woman because my brother probably wanted me around and asked why I was not there also. I felt she literally "hated me" because I know my brother looked to me to protect him in some way and he knew I loved him.. Even though I feel I let him down by deserting him and going home two different times. As I pondered about my treatment,(as I am writing) I also wondered if he was angry with me for leaving him on the island with her or he was the one who didn't want me around. Even though I don't believe the later was the reason.*

For years, in all her letters she always wrote how my brother cared about me, but that must have really caused her to feel less loved by him in some way).

FIX-UP

Gilda tried to 'fix up" my mother with a date with a soldier. Mother did not like that and she asked me to stay close to her and not leave her side for any reason. Finally, the soldier got the idea that although a friendly person, mother just was not interested in him and he just left.

(*Today, knowing what I know about Gilda, I believe this was her attempt to discredit my mother so she would be called unfit, but she was unsuccessful because Mother and I stayed together until he left the house never to be seen again. Mother although both passive and naive, was tremendously loyal and faithful to Dad.)*

THE FIRE

Mother put my sister to bed and we were all downstairs. Mother always checked on her and when she was walking up the stairs she smelled smoke and yelled for me to come. She went into the bedroom first and said, "Marlys your sister's head is locked between the posts on the bed. You pull hard on both of them and I will pull her head out." We were both relieved as we worked together and got her out..

The light she had left on was very bright and Mother had put a towel over the light to darken the room. The towel caught fire and was smoldering. The room was filled with smoke but it was billowing mostly up high.

Mother said, "Quick soak some towels in the tub and bring them to me." She pulled the smoldering towel off the light and threw it on the floor. Then, she picked up my sister and we met at the door. She told me to take my sister, put her on the bathroom floor while she took the wet towels and put out the fire. I don't think she ever told anyone about this incident because Gilda would have made a big issue about it..

MOTHER DECIDES TO GO HOME

Mother took me aside and told me she needed to go back to Minnesota with Dad. She talked to me for a long time very concerned about Craig and I. She told me she really needed me to stay and please watch over my brother Craig. I did not want to stay but agreed to do what Mother requested. Mother and Cheryl left for Minnesota. She knew I would keep watch over him as I did so often when we were younger. We (Mother, Craig and I) would go for walks and my brother would decide that he did not want to go the way we were going and be very obstinate. She would say, "Come on Marlys let's just go on home and leave him here." Those words put panic in my soul and I just wouldn't leave him. Instead I would go to him and convince him any way I could to come along with me. After a little pulling and begging he would finally come with me.

I really did not want to stay in California with this frightening woman whom I did not trust, like or feel safe with, but my passive nature could only obey the wish of my mother, so I agreed to stay a few months. I continued to be alone most of the time. I hardly ever saw my brother. I learned later the reason given for me to stay was that there was a polio epidemic. Mother wanted to take all of us back to Minnesota but Gilda had convinced her it was safer for us in California and "promised" we both would return to them next summer. Within a few months it proved to be too long a time for me and by Christmas I was lonely for my parents and home.

CELEBRITIES

I remained behind and every weekend celebrities came to the house. This always led to some kind of party with houseguests staying until all hours of the night. Anyone that had anything to do with movies fascinated me. I really loved the movies of those days and some of these people were so much fun to see and meet, if only for a few minutes.

One visit was from Rudy Valle, an older man who had red hair who was a crooner of his day. Another was a movie magazine and gossip columnist May Mann. Another party, actor Johnny Warburton and his actress wife and John Sutton, actor in the movie "Saratoga Trunk" were her cocktail hour guests. Another time Sylvia Sidney and Arthur Lake and his wife. Evidently she gave good parties and people enjoyed coming.

It was fun listening to their stories but my time with them was always limited. All of these people were nice to me and it was so much fun listening to their stores and hearing them talk about other stars and famous people I had seen in movies or read about in magazines. Gilda always cut my time short. I think she was afraid that they might learn the truth about my brother. I was smart enough to realize that if I said anything, I would dearly pay for it. Even at that young age I understood when to keep my mouth shut!

LEFT ALONE ON THE STREET

Gilda was the opposite of my mother in every sense of the word. She had no motherly instincts that gave her a sense of responsibility for a child's welfare and certainly not for mine at any time at all. She asked me if I wanted to go out with her and then she would just drop me off someplace. I was told to "Get out of the car and wait for her to pick me up later!"

One time she took me and left me for two hours at a dime store while she did something else. I was terrified. I had to go to the bathroom, but was afraid to leave the front of the dime store for fear she would come by, not find me and just leave me. Why did she want to torment me like this?

I tried to keep myself busy watching people passing by. I did not have any money to buy anything so I just stood and waited outside the store. Tears flowed from my eyes and I felt so alone. People who walked by just looked at me, but no one approached and asked if they could help me.

Finally hours later at dusk, the limousine arrived and she picked me up. My parents never would have done such a thing to any child. Once I was back home and secure again, I never was asked about my visit and I never told about the abuse I felt was done to me.

Another time she had the chauffer just drop me off all by myself at a movie theater. When the movie was over I waited and waited. Night fell and people just looked at me. I think I began to cry then too, I didn't know what to do. They forgot all about me. The lady in the ticket box asked me some questions. I think that from what I told her, she located a phone number and called the house. I was so scared. Finally, the chauffeur came and picked me up and said he was sorry I had to wait so long.

(As I reflect during the writing I have become acutely aware of *the damage done to my spirit. Over and over again this woman "wounded" my spirit and thwarted emotional development. What had she done to my little brother Craig? Did she leave him unattended causing fears and scars in his life?. From his demeanor as an adult male, obviously something was done to hurt him tremendously.*

While staying in California, I led a pretty lonely existence, going to school, walking home alone, doing my homework, listening to the radio, walking around the three acres of land and just day dreaming. I would think about home and the wonderful times I had spent with my four grandparents. I wanted to be with them again, enjoy them, have good food and laughter as we played games together.

Remembering the Good Times at Home

Dad's Old Car

Grandpa Johnsen & Dad

– Marlys and Craig –
The Neighbor Kids & us.

REFLECTING ON VISITS WITH OUR GRANDPARENTS

Craig and I enjoyed visits with our Swedish and Norwegian grandparents. We especially enjoyed Christmas and the wonderful

Scandinavian cooking. The best part was all the love we received every time we were with them.

Our childhood visits were always filled with laughter and joy. We usually took turns going to either the paternal or maternal grandparents homes. We spent wonderful hours learning card games like fish and rummy or Chinese checkers. Sometimes we would go fishing in one of Minnesota's ten thousand lakes, spend all day out in the middle of the lake and come home and have fried fish for dinner. Grandmother Johnsen loved to put breadcrumbs out for the birds and she would let us throw them. We loved swinging on the summer swing in the back yard or the small one hanging from the rafters in the basement during the winter months. Her neighbor Mrs. Duseck had an apple tree and sometimes after we asked permission, we were allowed to get up in it and pick some apples. Both grandmothers would love to make special treats for us. Grandmother Johnsen would have homemade jelly, canned peaches or pears.

Our other grandmother Hultgren would treat us with delicious pastry or root beer floats. Mornings she would serve the pastry and something warm. She would let me have coffee with lots of cream and sugar and let me dip my roll or donut into it. It was yummy good! Summer nights the windows were left open and we could hear the chirping crickets and the streetcars passing by. Lights would dance across the bedroom ceiling. We deeply loved all our grandparents and we felt their love for us as well.

GRANDPARENTS ROOTS

Our Mother's mother came from Sweden when she was only twelve years old. She came through Canada and arrived at her brother's home in Minneapolis on a Sunday. Everyone was at a picnic in the park because they had no idea when she would arrive. A nice lady helped her find their home.

Grandmother only went to the fourth grade but she self-educated herself while she worked in exclusive girls school. When she first came to America. She especially enjoyed every display of proper manners. She had a wonderful enthusiasm for learning proper English and her spelling was exceptional. She was a wonderful homemaker, mother and cook. In the school she helped with the cooking and cleaning to earn her room and board. It was here that she learned proper etiquette and how to set an elegant dinner table. Grandmother and Grandfather Hultgren met in a youth meeting at church. He came with his parents as a young child from Sweden. Grandfather Hultgren's father was a Swedish Methodist-Episcopal minister. He traveled the circuit on a horse and buggy throughout Minnesota, Wisconsin and Michigan ministering to the Swedish immigrants and finally settled in Minnesota. Grandfather was educated and loved poetry. He had many poems memorized and he had a delightful mind and spirit. It came alive as he recited it to us as children. When we visited he would take us to the park and swing us on the swing or watch while we played on the merry-go-round. When the radio was playing music, he would tap his fingers to the beat. He spent his life loving everyone he met along life's pathway. He worked as a postal clerk sorting mail in the Minneapolis Post Office until he retired. He also sold life insurance and collected premiums part time. Later he was a courier for a pharmaceutical firm. He did this to increase his Social Security so they would remain independent and not be a burden to his children. He would have been a terrific educator in English literature or even a preacher, but I guess times were pretty hard during the depression years. Just working to feed his family of four children, Marion, Mildred (our mother), Milton and Louise was a struggle during the depression.

Dad's Mother was a wonderful mother, grandmother and homemaker too. She loved to garden and she grew lovely vegetables and flowers. She was a good seamstress and she would sew for some affluent people in Minneapolis in her day. She also enjoyed cleaning other people's homes, play bridge, worship and serve in her church. Grandpa and Grandma Johnsen had a lot of Norwegian friends and they enjoyed playing cards and socializing together. Grandpa and Grandma met in Norway. Her mother was a terrific seamstress and Grandma went to work on Grandpa's family farm. Grandpa worked for the Great Northern Railroad. (I wrote a separate fantasy love story called "Love Began in the Fjords" recalling a few facts about them but not using their names.)

BACK TO REALITY…I AM ALONE IN CALIFORNIA

The Dahlberg mansion in Beverly Hills was built on about three to five acres of land. The house stood on the side of a hill and with the pool area below. Below the pool was a chicken coup and a lot of chickens wandering around. The chickens were fun to watch and feed. I was allowed to collect the eggs and bring them to the kitchen. I didn't go swimming in the large pool unless there were adults around because I did not know how to swim. I had a fear of drowning.

Gilda kept Craig and I pretty much separated and we didn't see each other that much even living in the same house. She would take him places after school but I was never privy to that information and she was with him most of the time or he would be off to a friend's home.

LOOKING FORWARD TO THE FANCY PARTY

They were going to have a fancy party with lots of celebrities. Gilda had me calling special people from a special phonebook she had marked. She instructed me to ask for the person and the exact words to say to them. I was to wait for an answer from the special guests on the list she wanted to attend. (*I wondered if they would take seriously an invitation from a child, but I did what I was asked to do. My reward was to see and meet some movie stars at the party.!)*

I considered the words as a promise to me for helping her. She knew how anxious I was to meet some famous movie stars. I had already met a few movie stars and I was so excited. The night of the party I got all dressed up in my very best dress, which had a velvet bodice and a multi-colored striped taffeta skirt. It was the dress that my grandmother had bought me and I thought I looked nice in it. A few guests arrived and the butler was making them drinks.

One guest was songwriter Sammy Kahn who instantly made friends with the beautiful grand piano and began to play some of the songs he had written. I was told he had a number one song of the year and his song was the title of a great film, "I'll Be Seeing You." I recognized the music and was so thrilled to meet a famous song writer. I loved music and wished that I knew how to play the piano like he did. We sat and listened as he played several of his songs.

Across from the piano were two chairs and one lady sitting looked very much like a star I recognized. I spoke to her and learned that she was the mother of Ginger Rogers. She was such a lovely woman and as I recall had a warm friendly voice as she talked with me. I sat beside her in the other chair. Then, I guess Gilda noticed we were talking too long a time and thought I was bothering her guests and she insisted that I go up to my bedroom. She said, "I promise I will call you later when more stars arrive." The obedient child that I was, I went upstairs and waited and waited. There was a small door just off her bedroom that held a balcony of potted plants overlooking one of the rooms. Before I lay down to wait for her to call me, I snuck over and peeked through the door to see if I could see anyone I recognized. Disappointed I went to my room and just waited until I finally just fell asleep. She had promised she would call me when more of the guests had arrived and she never woke me. Gilda broke her word to me, something my parents would never do. My parents honored whatever they said and their word was gold because whatever they promised, they did! They taught me that keeping promises was important in relationships with others. Today I hold any promise in high regard whether it is one I make or one made to me.

In the morning, I was super hurt and disappointed at not having met some movie stars and politely expressed my feelings to her. She just passed it off as nothing. I was insulted. "How could she? Something she knew really meant a lot to me. She just laughed at me. I felt as if I didn't belong here anymore. My brother had his little friends but I had no one. The colored servants Zike and Evelyn were always nice to me but they weren't family.

I really missed my parents about six weeks after mother left. What happened really was the last straw for me and I wrote home that I was unhappy and I wanted to go home too. I wrote a letter and gave it to my uncle to mail. The woman somehow got hold of it, and opened it up and read it. She probably expected to read what a wonderful time I was having. Within days Gilda shook the letter in front of my face and asked in a very harsh and cruel manner "What is this all about? You are unhappy here? You ungrateful child." and then she said,. "After all I have done for your family, how on earth could I be unhappy?" She literally scared the voice right out of my mouth and I could hardly speak. I wanted to cry because I was not an ungrateful person. I had never had my mother speak to me in this tone of voice. I tried to reply honestly, that I was lonesome and I just wanted to go home! Her body language told me she was very angry with me and no matter what I said would have been wrong in her eyes. I had never observed anyone so out of control! My uncle was present and did not say a word to protect me from her. I decided he was also afraid of her as I was. *(My question now is, "What did she have on him that he didn't want anyone to know about?"*

Why didn't he come to my defense? He was my favorite uncle but he didn't stick up for me in any shape or form. Years later, I wonder of what real help was he ever to my parents who entrusted their son to Gilda because of his presence in the home.}

GOING HOME

Hardly a day went by before I was told I was going home for Christmas. Then Gilda said, "Pack your things" and before you could shake a stick, I was extracted from the house, driven in the limousine to the Los Angeles train station. I was dropped off all by myself and without money for food. The chauffeur gave a tip to a kind Redcap who took me to a chair to sit and wait. He watched and cared for me and took me to my train when it finally arrived six hours later. This was a week before Christmas. Once again I was left alone in the great big city of Los Angeles and so scared. I was too scared to even move from my spot and go to the bathroom. I had my things packed in one suitcase and a cardboard box tied with a string. I didn't dare just leave them or someone might take my things. The Redcap would stop by periodically and let me know he was around. I wish I could thank that Redcap today. I'm sure God gave him a special reward in heaven for caring for this lonely and frightened child.

I spent four days on the train because of bad weather and I had only the $2.00 that mother had given me before she left. I went to the diner car to get something to eat the first day, but I could not even afford a sandwich. I did not know what to do. One time someone must have realized I hadn't eaten and gave me a cookie. A young Wave who asked if she might share my berth and rest and give me something to eat, or I would have gone without food during the whole trip.

Bedtime came and we climbed in the berth. Hours later, I woke to a lot of movement only to realize that there was another person also in the bed and the Wave was having sex with him. I felt trapped as I was near the window; so I just lay there and waited until it stopped. Finally all quieted down and I went to sleep.

On top of everything there was a big snowstorm and the train was delayed in Kansas City an extra day. I sat and looked out the window silently staying in my own little world most of the trip. Mile by mile I was heading in the right direction, to a place called "home".

I never told anyone about the young Wave when I got home. I felt ashamed to even know about and actually be in such a situation. In fact, I never told anyone until years and years later when I told my mother and all she did was laugh. It was too late to do anything about it and I think she was embarrassed. I didn't think it was funny! Probably had I told someone earlier, they would have at least chastised Gilda for her lack of motherly instinct to see a child had money for food and drink, least of all no chaperone for a young child on a long trip across the country.

HOME SWEET HOME

Finally arriving home late at night or early in the morning, I was so glad to see the faces of my Mother and Dad as I walked off the train. My grandparents and aunt were there too. They looked so wonderful to me. Once again I felt "safe and secure" as they put their arms around me. I hoped I would never experience separation from them ever again.

(As I reflected, I wonder what my brother must have felt like when all of a sudden— I deserted him once again. I did not even have a chance to say goodbye to him. A darling little boy left alone with someone who was neither mother nor family. Psychologically everything that had happened to Craig was already unbelievable and now I left him stranded again. Once again the pangs of guilt touched me and I felt guilty for being "home" and that guilt has never left me to this day. Even as I write about this my eyes tear up and my heart fills with emotion. I was able to share this with my mother the last year of her life and she said she never knew that I felt that way and I shouldn't have. But children see things so differently than adults and take on responsibility that really does not belong to them.

Living with this woman who had so much wealth, I felt unloved, rejected and abused. It is unfortunate I was such a quiet obedient child because I never told anyone, not even my parents all the things that happened to me. My brother couldn't tell anyone either and I often wonder what "all" really did happen to him.)

I had written a note and much to my surprise a few weeks after going home I received this note from Gilda. It read:

(Like most of her letters, this one is filled with flowery words, half-truths and empty promises. She wanted everyone to love her so much and sadly was truly loved only by her family.)

Dear Marlys,

I just found your note this morning, and it was a wonderful surprise. Your handwriting is beautiful and so is your painting.

I saw the paintings you did while here and you have a real artist's talent. Now I am looking forward to hearing you sing – several people told me you have a lovely voice. How would you like to study singing and art in California? I would love to send you to some fine teachers there if your Mother and Daddy are willing.

You can become a very successful artist if you start your training soon. And Bror would be so proud of you, too – you know he has always wanted to have you near him as you are a special favorite of his.

So we all have a lot of happiness to look forward to – here's hoping we all be in California and can work and play together and I hope you will all be at Red Crest soon so you can build up for the fall and winter and so I can get you a pretty wardrobe of clothes and reward for being such a good daughter to your mother and father.

Loads of love and a big kiss from your pal,(signed) Gilda.

PART II

EXCUSES…EXCUSES.

World War II is in full bloom. Food is scarce and we have food-rationing stamps for everything, especially meat, we purchase at the grocery store. We take the left over grease to the meat department as part of the war effort. We have air raid tests and everyone turned off their lights. Daddy is an air raid warden and he left us during those hours at night. It is a scary world for little children living in any part of the world even though in America, we did not have bombs dropping around us.

Our parents continued to make repeated requests for the Dahlbergs to return my brother home. Their attempts failed and our parents were frustrated with the Dahlbergs for not keeping their promise. When mother's sister Louise and her husband Eddie were in California they stopped to visit Craig in Beverly Hills. According to their report Craig was in good health. Days before Mom and Dad received a letter that Craig was too ill to travel and return home. Hearing Mother and Dad they made another request to bring Craig home. Only to again receive another excuse that they should not take him out of school until the end of the semester. Then, another time it was that he was looking forward to a visit with a special friend.

Craig – Gilda – Ed – Louise – Uncle Milton

Gilda & Craig (below)

Arthur Lake's Son (above)
"Dagwood"

Gilda and both Boys

Milton and Craig

It continued over and over again throughout the summer and the fall weather was settling in again.

During these years Gilda would send my parents telegrams, $5.00 certificates at Saks Fifth Avenue (never used) for Mother's day from Craig. Periodically she would write letters about how healthy and happy he was in California. Mom and Dad wanted him returned home but she wanted my brother as "her possession." She claimed it was her generosity yet, she included every single item worked for and/or given to every member of our family later in a lawsuit against my parents.

MOTHER DECIDES SHE HAS WAITED LONG ENOUGH

It was November and Mother could not stand it any longer and with the financial help of her parents they made arrangements for her to go to California and bring Craig back home. Mother was a small woman with a quiet and gentle spirit and for her to muster up enough determination and courage to go alone was a big decision. She traveled by train for three days and during that time she did a lot of praying. She asked God how she was going to handle this very difficult woman who had refused to bring her child home as promised.

Knowing Mother, fear was a constant companion, but "when love takes charge—fear has a tendency to take second place." Tears flowed freely from mother's eyes as she sat on the train anticipating what might take place. Love for her son gave her the courage to do what she needed to do. It would have been easier on her if Dad could have come along but he felt an obligation to stay and provide for the family by continuing to work. When the train arrived in Los Angeles, she got her bag and took a cab to the Dahlbergs home in Beverly Hills.

Mother rang the doorbell and the servants came to the door and ushered her into the entry hall and announced her arrival to Gilda. Gilda came down utterly surprised asking, "Why are you here?" Mother replied, "I am here to pick up my son and take him home. Where is he?" Outraged, Gilda told her, "Under no certain terms are you going to do any such thing." and slapped Mother in the face! She pushed Mother backward and Mother almost lost her balance. Mother was shocked and did not retaliate because it was not in her nature to do such a thing.

(That slap was so hard it broke the veins in Mother's cheek and the mark remained apparent the rest of life. She had to cover it with makeup to hide its appearance and a constant reminder of that dreadful event.)

Mother could see the rage in the Gilda's dark eyes. About that time Craig hearing the commotion appeared in the room and ran to Mother. She threw her arms around him and gave him a great big hug and kiss telling him how much she missed him. She could hardly believe what was happening or what was said to her. Fear for her self and her son gripped her insides, but she did not want her son to get upset, so she remained outwardly calm and controlled her actions. Later when she was alone and out of the ear range the tears came. What was she going to do? She prayed realizing she was now possibly trapped and guarded in Gilda's house. Mother asked for God's help mustering up the faith of a tiny mustard seed. Mother had never encountered a strong personality like Gilda before and her passive nature had kicked in.

After a little while, Gilda seemed to calm down. She must have noticed Craig's loving and excited response to Mother's arrival. After thinking things over (or possibly she telephoned her attorney) Gilda realized her own situation and that she had no legal right. Bror was home and he always had a calming affect on the events surrounding his wife. Gilda knew Mother had all the rights in the world to take their son home at any time.

Just as quickly as all of her rage and hate exploded so spontaneously, she began to pour on the kindness and welcomed Mother to stay for a "visit" and see her son. She instructed the servants to show Mother a room. Both Mom and Craig were now prisoners of this ruthless woman who wanted to keep Craig as her own son.

Gilda informed the servants and the chauffeur that *my brother was not to leave the premises.* And Mother was also notified she was not to leave with Craig to go anywhere! The chauffeur even let it be known that he carried a gun and Mother summarized that this was done to scare her. It did! That night Mother spent most of the night praying hard, asking God for help and an idea of how she was going to carry out her plans to take her son home. It became very obvious these people had no intention of letting her take her own son anywhere.

As Mother lay awake praying, "all of a sudden" an idea came to her. Her uncle was choir director at a church and she would take her son to church on Sunday and seek his help. She called him on the telephone and told him that she hoped she could go to church on Sunday.

Sunday was approaching and things seemed to calm down a bit. Mother was not allowed to leave or go anywhere with my brother. Finally the time seemed right and she found the courage and asked permission to take him to church where her uncle was choir director and the Dalbergs agreed to allow this, giving specific instructions to the chauffeur. It was miraculous how God blinded this woman's mind so the plan could take place and Mother was allowed to take her son away.

When Sunday morning arrived, Mother asked the (gun-carrying) chauffeur to take her and my brother to church. When they arrived at the church the chauffeur waited in the car. After the service was over she rushed forward and told her Uncle George (church choir director) and the family what had happened and that the chauffeur had a gun. He said, "We will leave quickly by the rear door."

They rushed Mother and my brother out through the rear entrance. When almost everyone had left the church, the chauffeur realized the church was nearly empty and that they had gone out by another exit. Watching for them, he spotted them leaving and in spite of the traffic, followed them to the uncle's home and began banging on the door. He shouted and threatened them. He left and called the Dahlbergs, who came with the police and continued to harass the family. The police told them they had no rights and to leave but they stayed around for hours.

Uncle George called his friend; Sam Yorty a very prominent Los Angeles attorney and he came and told the man to leave. They called my Dad and he flew out to California to accompany Mother and my brother home. The attorney explained to them, that they had no legal rights here and could not take a child from his Mother. Then arrangements were made for Mom and Dad to leave Los Angeles as quickly as possible.

Legally the Dahlbergs had no grounds to stand on and Gilda gave Mother's uncle a very hard time with loud yelling and screaming. Gilda remained there all night yelling threats, banging on windows and doors, so no one could sleep. They learned their telephone wires had also been cut.

Before Gilda left, she said to mother's uncle, "You will pay for this." (Remember! If you disagreed with her will… she always found a way to cause you further irritation to get her revenge) According to the first wife of Uncle Milton, he had become an emotional bond slave to Gilda and even found papers Gilda had made him sign indicating he was "not a free person", whatever that meant!. He also had become dependant of the rich lifestyle and use of alcohol, which became his lifetime companion and enemy that destroyed his life and ultimately killed him.

Mother, Dad and Craig arrived home safely but there was now an air of fear and oppression that penetrated our lives. We didn't know what to expect next. My brother was enrolled back in school in Minneapolis. I was told to never leave him on the way to or from school or anytime an adult member family was not around. For a little girl of ten or eleven years old, this was an awesome responsibility. Mother would walk all the way to school and meet us to be sure we were safe. She took over most of the time but we would start out from school by ourselves.

Christmas came and our little family seemed to be back to normal. My brother was so happy to be home with us and we believed that all was well.

It was snowing and all the children were outside making a big snowman. Mother told us that tonight was the night my brother and I would go with Dad to pick out a Christmas tree. This was an annual event we always looked forward to as the holiday approached. Dad pulled us on the sled to the nearby Christmas tree lot and it was so much fun.

Dad worked hard and most other evenings he came home after we were in bed. Tonight was special, Dad came home early and dinner was ready. Mother called us in to wash our hands and get ready for dinner. Before we had even begun to eat our dinner, excitedly my brother asked, "When can we go pick out the tree?" Dad was a man who always did what needed to be done at his own pace without a lot of confusion. You could count on his word that he would do exactly what he said he would do but as little children we had not learned that about him as yet.. Dad explained that we had plenty of time and he wanted to finish dinner. We were to wait patiently for him.

Our eyes became fixed on our Daddy's plate. We gobbled up our dinner as fast as possible and were excused from the table. We couldn't really figure out why it took Dad so long to finish his meal. Finally Daddy was finished, but did not seem in much of a hurry. Then, he finally called, "Children, I am ready to go". We were listening to some program on the radio. We scurried around putting on mittens and snowshoes and an extra scarf to put around our noses, because it seemed to get colder during the nighttime hours.

Daddy pulled out the sled and told us to sit on it. The snow was extra deep so Daddy had to walk down the path that the car tires had made in the snow. Heavy snow meant that Daddy had to tug a bit harder to get the sled with its passengers moving. Finally we arrived at the tree lot, and began looking around for just the right tree. Daddy always loved to get the tallest tree possible at Christmas, which meant that it really didn't fit well on the small sled. Of course the tree always got the ride home. We had to 'tag along' just as fast as our little legs would go to keep up with Dad.

When we arrived home, Dad would cut the tree to fit into the stand and bring it into the house. Mother decided where it was to be placed and assisted Dad to be sure the trunk was straight. When the lights were in place the electricity turned on. Dad would stand and analyze the situation. If all were well, he would make favorable sounds (Um Hum) and stand with pride of a job well done. He would praise "our" wonderful selection of a tree. That always bewildered me because Daddy always had the final word about the selection. Mother would just smile. Whatever Dad did was just fine with her. She brought out the boxes of ornaments and we all began to trim the tree. When the ornaments were on the tree, it was time for the tinsel. Mother and Dad had a special way it was to be put on and we were told to just sit down and watch. . Evidently, we children did not do it correctly! We just sat and watched Mom and Dad admiring our newly decorated tree. When they finished, Mother would put a clean-ironed sheet under the tree. It made the tree look like it was standing in snow.

Sometime before morning, Mother would place several presents under the tree. I remember my brother being anxious to learn which ones were his. He would ask and then seemed to get enjoyment out of shaking them and guessing what was in them.

Christmas Eve arrived and the space under the tree was full of beautifully wrapped gifts for everyone. The spirit of generosity and love prevailed in our family and I picked up on it quickly from an early age, I used my little allowance to get gifts for everyone. It wasn't much, but sharing what I had was important to me.

Those days it was the thought or sentiment that you were remembered that was important and it was an expression of our love for one another. The price of the gifts was unimportant. (For me, this is still what I believe. "Being loved and remembered" is what really counts. Somehow that tells me I am loved and cared about)

OUR FAVORITE HOLIDAY IS HERE….CHRISTMAS EVE

We always celebrated Christmas Eve with our Swedish grandparents. Grandpa did not drive a car and it was easier for us to go to their home than for them to take a streetcar with packages to our home. Grandmother was a wonderful Swedish cook and we enjoyed a delicious meal. Her table was graced formally with crystal goblets, china, linen and silver. It was a time we learned proper etiquette and about formal dining.

After dinner we opened our gifts and there was always one special gift from our grandparents. One year I received a beautiful pressed glass perfume bottle (I still have it) and that Christmas holds special memories for me. I was recognized as a young lady and it made me feel very special. Another Christmas my brother received a red wagon. We used that wagon many times in the years to come. One time when I was very sick with impetigo and we had to go to the doctor. Mother pulled us both for miles to get there because Dad was working and she did not drive..

When Christmas evening was over, we had to go home to await the great event of Santa's arrival. My brother fell asleep and Daddy had to carry him to the car. It seemed like a long trip home during the cold winter night but actually it was less than five miles.. The streets were icy and snow billowed down as we rode along. Our old 1928

Stud baker was cold with no heater, but we always carried an extra blanket to keep us warm. Both of our grandparents lived in North Minneapolis and we lived in South Minneapolis and it probably was a twenty-minute drive but it seemed much longer.

CHRISTMAS MORNING SANTA ARRIVES

Santa arrived during the night and we woke up to 'unwrapped' gifts for each of us from the Saint of the Christmas, left under or near the Christmas tree. Whatever Santa left, it was always something we really wanted and had asked Santa for when we visited him at the store during the holidays. Mother and Dad felt that one gift was sufficient from him because whoever gave us 'other gifts' deserved the appreciation of a "thank you" from us. *I happened to agree with that philosophy and when we had our daughter, we continued the custom. This kept Santa in his proper place, teaching Christmas is not all about just receiving gifts but giving them as well. Christmas is about remembering the true meaning of Christmas and the birth of Jesus Christ, the Messiah/Savior who was born on that day. He is the one we remember, love and celebrate by sharing gifts, because that is what the wise men did to honor Him.*

CHRISTMAS DAY AT GRANDPARENTS

Christmas day we always went to the Dad's parents' home, and again had a wonderful meal and opened more presents. The aroma of a Norwegian Christmas dinner was in the air and it was always a day to remember. We enjoyed more delicious food. Sometimes Grandpa and Grandma would talk to each other in Norwegian during the meal. I often wondered what they were saying. After dinner, we would open gifts. The radio was turned on and lovely Christmas music filled the air. They were very practical people and liked to give us pajamas or slippers. One year, Grandmother knitted a lovely sweater for me, which I really enjoyed wearing for many years. Their home was always warm and cozy and they always had a tree that went to the ceiling, a tradition my own father loved.

When we arrived home, our Dad tucked us into bed and Mother made some coffee and serve holiday cookies to dad and her self. Dad turned on the radio and they listened to some music before retiring to their bed.

RESTRAINING ORDER

However, January arrived and the wealthy couple filed a restraining order against my parents, saying that they had not rehabilitated my brother and his health was in jeopardy, living at home with us. They noted in the document doctors names, opinions, dates, times and places; amounts of monies they had spent on Craig's behalf. (*All out of the goodness of their hearts. Unbelievable isn't it?)*

The folk's attorney in Los Angeles (Sam Yorty) responded, telling the Dahlbergs that they had no legal right to the Craig, and my parents had all the legal rights. This must have enraged the woman because her hate and venom festered and obviously from what happens next she began to plot her next invasion and abuse of our lives.

(Our loving, forgiving parents never realized at that time what was really happening with her insidious and obsessive fascination with my little brother. Their naivety was truly enveloped in their own innocence. Gilda was ultimately going to cause us much more trouble. Sadness still fills my heart remembering how my brother was cheated of being a part of our family and enjoying the love we all shared celebrating holidays and birthdays with parents, grandparents, and aunt and uncles. Enjoying the traditional Scandinavian food and celebrations at Christmas, Thanksgiving, Easter and Birthdays.)

FEARS AND DREAMS

During these years we just had a radio to get the news reports. It was bad enough as a child hearing about the second world war and hundreds of people dying in Europe. What I heard really stimulated my imagination and I would have horrible dreams about being places where the war was taking place. One dream I had still remains a part of my memories that frightened me.

WORLD WAR II ENDS

The boys are coming home! Within weeks all my uncles would be coming home and we would be at peace again in the world. When we heard the news that the war had ended we were sitting at the dinner table. I remember my Daddy and Mother having the happiest expressions on their faces that I had really not seen since Craig was /taken from us. Even as a child the news of the wars end gave me a sense of relief. No more frightening dreams either.

(Obviously hindsight always lends insight to what took place next. The unscrupulous and manipulative mind of this woman was activated to get her way again. It is hard to believe that when events unfold that Gilda merely acted impulsively like a spoiled child. Yet, giving her the benefit of the doubt, that might have been what it was.

Regardless anyone's selfishness is always at the price of another.)

Soon our family was to be Traumatized the Second Time – Brother is Kidnapped!

A "SURPRISE" VISIT FROM THE WEALTHY WOMAN and the "KIDNAPPING"

It was a very hot July day and we were playing paper dolls on the sun porch when up drove a dark green limousine and the exotic wealthy "Gilda" with a little girl named Bonnie walked up to our front door and rang the door bell. Bonnie was Gilda's husbands granddaughter and about two years old. Several months had passed without incident. Kind letters and telegrams had arrived from the woman. Mother was caught totally off guard trusting and never expecting what was to happen next! Surprised herself and not realizing the cunningness of this woman, she welcomed Gilda with acceptance and warmth. She invited her to stay for lunch and sent me to the grocery store. While she was in the kitchen Gilda was asking Craig to go for a ride with her. Our parents were very good people, always forgiving and kind and willing to let bygones be bygones. But bad things do happen to good people!

Craig and I had several of our little friends over and we were playing together when she arrived. I was playing paper dolls with friends on the front sun porch and Craig was fiddling on the piano with his little friend. Gilda was intensively watching Craig and admiring his so-called artistic talents while talking to Mother.

All of a sudden Gilda said, "The children are so hot, wouldn't you all like some nice cold ice cream?" Of course, they all said, "Yes"

Then she said, "I want to get them something cool and refreshing. I will go get them all some ice cream at the store." It was hot and we all thought that it was a great idea. She said, "I need the children to ride along and show me where the store is". *There were three stores only one block away, yet as an adult she couldn't go with a chauffer?*

It all happened so quickly and our Mother was totally taken off guard by what she thought was the kind actions of this woman. When Gilda motioned for my brother, a neighbor girl and my little sister Cheryl, as she picked baby Bonnie to accompany her and show her the way to the store. Mother did not stop her—believing they would all be right back. As she left, she assured mother by saying, "We will be back in just a few minutes." Everyone piled into the big fancy green limousine.

She took the neighbor girl named Nancy, sister Cheryl (see the copy of her letter with legal papers in the back of this story) my brother Craig and little Bonnie into the limousine with her masseuse named "Doc" and drove off. When they got to the corner—- she told her chauffeur to stop. She then told the neighbor girl, "Get out of the car."

Shocked and frightened, Nancy carrying my sister ran back to our house and yelling loudly telling our mother. "The woman "kidnapped Craig and he wanted to get out of the car too and he began to cry". (*Her affidavit is at the end of the book.)*

Mother could hardly believe what had happened and began to cry and cry. Her son was gone again. Mother was frantic. She called Daddy and he rushed home.

(I believe Gilda was showing Mother, she could take Craig off too, just as Mother had done in California. She was getting back at my parents for talking to her husband Bror and insisting Craig, be returned home. She was going to prove what "power and money" could do! She wanted a little darling boy child and she "Kidnapped my brother"!

Unfortunately, some people having money and influence can break the laws of our land and get away with it! It is a mockery of our justice system! How can there be justice in injustice?

THE RIDE NORTH

Knowing the character of this woman and the temperament of my brother. I can now vision what took place in that limousine. During the ride north, she tried to cuddle my brother Craig and hold him tight and told him a bunch of stories to get his mind off what had just happened. He was extremely frightened having been taken away from his Mother and sister. I can see him holding his body stiffly to resist her. His anger and/or fear might have even caused him to kick, bite or hit her.

She didn't care about the trauma she was putting Craig through or even the lasting damage it would cause him emotionally.

Once again she was separating him from his natural parents. It would have a lasting affect on his total life and affect his future development as a man. I am sure that she professed her love for him. Telling him she was taking him for his own good. She continued to tell him they were going for ice cream and would return to his house in a while. When he began to cry she tried to comfort him until his tears of an eight hour drive finally caused him to go to sleep. Possibly she even drugged him with something to quiet him if this was an actual plan she thought out ahead of time.

Later, You will see that in some way we don't understand or know, he became a slave to her desires, and he was helpless to leave her. Craig was emotionally helpless to leave her even when he was an adult to return home to his natural parents, who had always hoped for that kind of eventual result and awaited his return for years.

This obsessed woman "took my brother illegally" without my parent's full consent. She overruled my parents' authority and I am sure against my brother's wishes as well. She filled his mind with everything else other than the truth and she did that every day of his life. She damaged the soul of this little boy and traumatized and jeopardized his wholesome development and relationship with his natural family. In my opinion she was wicked and evil, motivated by her lust for what belonged to another. The deep seeded emotional problem of my brother's spirit is one he was never able to ever fully weed out or understand. Lies upon lies, deception at its worst imposed on a small child and it continued throughout his adult life.

A NEW NIGHTMARE FOR ALL OF US

Mother gasped with unbelief and her heart was filled with an extreme sense of pain having her son taken and stripped from her once again. The pain must have been closely related to that of childbirth or the death of someone you dearly love taken from you. Mother frantically telephoned Dad at work and told him what had happened. Immediately he came home and made plans to pursue her and get my brother.

After Dad came home, he called my uncle Gus, a neighbor Walter Julian and they took off for northern Minnesota to Red Crest or Swordfish island to get my brother. The police were called and the 'kidnapping' was reported. It seems to me someone connected to the police did tell Dad that the limousine was seen going north towards Canada. Those days a limousine was rarely seen on Minnesota streets or highways. I can only imagine Dad speeding up a two-lane highway to try to overtake the fancy limousine.

(Why my parents did not press "kidnapping charges" against her and have her arrested on the spot is beyond my comprehension. All I do know that my Dad would rather settle anything by "peaceful means" than have any kind of nasty confrontation and that is the way he lived his total life. My parents were always concerned how events would affect us children. I am sure that always remained some kind of factor in their decisions.)

I remember my mother trying to remain as calm as possible for my sister's and my sake. She gave us a sense of routine in spite of the circumstances. Inside—I am sure the emotion was like a tremendous storm. I could sense the depth of her emotion, but I was helpless to do anything or even fully understand what was taking place. I wanted to cry but I couldn't and I was scared, so very scared. I had years of nightmares because of what happened to my brother.

(Years later, I often wondered if my brother remembered the incident and how it affected him. Did he remember what Gilda had done to him or had fate blanked out his mind to all the traumatic

events she created that day and many other days ahead. Possibly his addictions helped him forget. I would have liked to talk to him about it, but there was never the opportunity! Either time wouldn't allow it or there were too many people around and our family pattern was always to be personal about such talks.

Our Daddy was a quiet and peaceful man, but I could see that this kind of thing caused him to experience a deep inner fear and anger and no one was going to take his son. Many years later, when my Dad was dying of cancer, he confessed to me his hatred for Gilda and I clearly understood why!

It saddens me that he had to live with so much hate in his heart and I know he was accountable to God for it—but I trust that a loving God knows all about it and also knows his heart. A death of a child would be devastating...but this was even so much worse.)

TRIP TO THE ISLAND

When they arrived in International Falls, my Dad rented a boat and they went to the island. They arrived at the island and surprised Gilda. When she saw Dad she attempted to hide my brother. Now, Dad was on "her turf". I am sure that whatever Daddy did, it was with caution not to alarm and traumatize my brother any further. He found Craig and took him to the boat.. She followed them.

On her own turf, she then proceeded to intimidate my Father. Yelling and screaming she said, "After all don't you appreciate all the things we have done for all of you?" *In our opinion, she did more harm that good!* She said, "What you are doing is wrong." Cunning in her way trying to convince him that she was right in all her actions of kidnapping Craig, and trying to intimidate and implicate Dad was in violation of something!

Finally, Dad got my brother in the boat to leave, and just at the last second as the boat was pulling away from the pier, the woman threw herself in the boat. Yelling and screaming, "You can't do this and reaching for Craig and saying that her husband would be arriving shortly." She made such a commotion rocking the boat that it presented a possibility that their lives were in danger. Dad tried to calm her down by saying, "Now lets talk this over quietly." Dad figured he could discuss what happened with Bror rationally, so he decided to go back to the island and wait for him to arrive. He sent the boat and his friends back to the main shore to wait for him. Bror arrived in a while. After explaining the kidnapping and why he was there, Mr. Dahlberg took Dad and my brother to the main shore. They all came back home.

WITHIN DAYS THE RICH LADY ARRIVES AT OUR DOOR AGAIN

After traumatizing our family, Gilda arrives all apologetic saying that she did not mean any harm to anyone. I don't actually remember her saying she was sorry for anything. When any one in our family would be apologetic, they were forgiven immediately. Sincerity was never questioned. Our home was always full of love and forgiveness. Taking full advantage of my parent's character and kindness she then acted as though she had done nothing to disrupt and traumatize our lives.

It was a bright March day when she arrived dressed in fur and riding in her fancy black limousine with chauffer. She was gushy nice and expressed love and affection for each of us. All smiles, her favorite word for everyone was "darling". Feeling accepted and forgiven she acted as though nothing had ever happened and all was well. She showed interest and spent time giving compliments to everyone. Mother fixed lunch while we children entertained her.

When she came, my friend Catherine and I were singing and dancing in our living room and I put on my one and only performance of a lifetime. I danced and sang like Betty Hutton who played in "Perils of Pauline". Why I wanted to impress this wealthy lady that I was somebody, I don't know? She raved how someday I could be a ballerina and dancer and commented how talented she thought I was. The crazy thing is that I wanted to believe her!

Gilda stayed for a long time talking with mother, my brother and myself. She asked if we might go to the island again this coming summer. After lunch she asked mother if she could take me shopping. Mother let me go! That surprised me and I wondered why me this time? Was she going to steal me off somewhere and Mother let her? We went in the big limousine to a store in downtown Minneapolis. We went to one of the big department stores to the second floor and she picked out a shiny black swimsuit, something she thought I would like. Actually the style was much too old for me and I never wore it. I dared not express my displeasure in her choice of gift for me. I don't know why she thought I needed a bathing suit.

In the limousine she talked constantly about going to the island for another summer vacation and how pretty I would look in the new bathing suit she had just purchased. We rushed from the store back to our house. In the car she proceeded to convince me that I wanted to return to Red Crest for another extended vacation and I was to bring my little friends along. I wondered if I was going to be taken from my parents like my brother had been taken before.

(However I didn't realize she was building on her "new plan to traumatize us further" and "purchased" my agreement to go to the island for the summer. Of course, I did not realize this at the time. Going along with her plan to take Craig from us the third time. She obviously did not want me!)

When we got back to the house, I remember my brother asking the fatal question. "How old was she?" She said, "I am 29 years old." She didn't get upset with him, which surprised me. I was old enough to realize that she was about 20 years our mothers senior and almost as old as our grandmothers. Our mother was about 30 years old!

This visit I remember Mother being very nervous but Mother was a very loving and forgiving person. A warm and hospitable person she treated her with respect because she was older. Gilda was a very authoritative powerful personality and it was hard to really carry on a conversation apart from her own agenda what ever it might be.

(This wealthy woman was a very cunning, possessive, domineering and determined person. Fearless to obtain what she wanted, disregarding the welfare and best interest of all concerned, as long as she could get her way!. She believed her cause is the right cause and had the finances to back her whims. She was arrogant and ruthless and believed she was above the law of man and God. Truth and honesty and respect had no rule in her life. I am sorry the folks didn't recognize she was the enemy sooner. They were very young and naïve).

As she bid us goodbye she took my brother in her arms and kissed him several times and said she loved him making a gushy display of affection far beyond what was normal or needed. My brother wiped the kisses away indicating that he didn't like it! When he was asked if he wanted to go to Red Crest Island again, Craig's reply was an emphatic "No". Gilda prodded him saying, "Marlys wants to go, don't you want to go with her and have a good time swimming and having fun?" At that Craig replied, "I will only go if Marlys goes with me." Gilda had already primed the pump well and succeeded in her goal to weave the web to take Craig away from his home and family again!

MY OPINION ABOUT THIS

In my opinion today, this was her way of getting back into the family's good graces. And as we know now, to set the scene for her next sinister move to tear our family apart. It was like Satan himself backing every evil insidious plan to separate our family. Her plan of revenge was still incomplete—- "over Daddy taking my brother back home."

Our parents did appreciate all the good things that she had done but at this point really did not believe all that was done was really necessary. Possibly that very attitude caused them to neglect doing some *of the things* that they should have, like putting her in jail for "kidnapping" Craig again and again. Traumatizing a small child in the way she did over and over again. All Craig needed was the loving care of his own family. These events caused them to begin to question Gilda's intentions as well as the health reports given to them.

He seemed to be a normal growing child to them. Note here: If he truly had as serious a problem as leukemia which they claimed, he probably would have died within a very few years..

WANTING THE BEST FOR THEIR CHILDREN

Dad wanted for his son what he was never able to get for himself. That was a good education. He held his dream as a high priority for his son. Because of his own early obligations with a wife and child, his own education was obtained through his hobby, which was reading. Self-educated, Dad could talk on almost any subject and probably could have answered any quiz question asked him. I admired my Father and his intelligence very much. Later in his life I felt he had much wisdom as well, probably gained from the suffering caused him in losing his son. He had a cruel and ruthless teacher— yet he remained a loving father and is to his honor.

Mother and Dad always were concerned about us kids being marred by these events and did their utmost to protect each one of us from it. Their remedy was to eliminate discussing these events with us or for that matter with anyone else. I doubt if they ever truly knew the serious and lasting affect it had on me. As a child, I could only assimilate what took place from my point of view.

My parents never argued or raised their voices. Our home was a very quiet and peaceful place and a healthy happy environment. The emotional affect of these traumatic events that happened with my brother and our family changed as I matured. With it came more questions of my parent's inability to change the course of events and why they fell prey to the wiles of these wealthy people in the first place.

Their money had too much power! When I was older, I could appreciate how very impossible it was for my parents and to put these events into proper prospective because it was so devastating. Again, I felt my own childlike pain but I also felt the pain of my parents and was helpless. Helpless not only at that moment they occurred, but also, for many years to come!

Opening a conversation about it with them usually was tolerated a few minutes and I was aware "pain" of all that had happened was revisiting them. Therefore, going any further than surface talk just didn't happen.

Aunt Marion and Uncle Gus
Their 25th Wedding Anniversary

GILDA HIRES AUNT AND UNCLE AS HOUSEHOLD HELP

Aunt Marion had lived with us for about a year and now her husband Gus would be coming home from the Navy. Gilda called and asked if they might like to work for her as caretakers on their island in the Lake of the Woods. She talked to Uncle Gus and he decided that would be an interesting job until he got settled down after the war so they agreed.

With our aunt and uncle at the island, how could my parents refuse letting us go there another summer? It was comforting to Mother and Dad, but they were both very busy doing servant duties, cooking, keeping the boats in working order, cleaning and keeping things in order they hardly had time to see much of either of us.

PART III

Invited for second vacation on the island. Again it ends sadly!

SECOND SUMMER INVITATION

My parents received another invitation for Craig and I to return to the island and to bring a friend with me. So plans were made and I made two trips back and forth with two of my friends. I didn't see my brother Craig very much and I was very pre- occupied with my friends and trips on the bus. Gilda was taking care of Craig.

I hadn't the slightest notion of what she did with him all day long.

My friends and I had a wonderful time wandering around the island; going places I had never been. We went across that rickety bridge and through the woods to the other side of the island where you could see Canada. At the time that seemed pretty exciting!

We took out the canoes and paddled between the islands. My friend kept urging me to go further and further away. I got scared because the winds were coming up and the water was getting choppy. I said, "I am going back" and she followed. It was certainly fun but very dangerous for a child that does not know how to swim. My friend did know how to swim so she probably knew she would be o.k. had the canoe tipped over, but I would have drown.

Another time between visits of the friends I took a rowboat out alone on to the lake. I stayed close to shore and then, a storm came up pulled me further out into the lake. I tried to row against the current but couldn't. I frantically yelled and yelled until someone heard me and took the speedboat out to rescue me. Before they got the boat back to the boathouse, it began to rain and I was drenched. Another valuable lesson learned! Have an adult with me and certainly ask before I would ever do that again!

On the few rainy days we were allowed to play the victorola in the dining room. Once a week, we took a trip to the small town of International Falls. There wasn't much to do so we usually just sat around and waited for everyone to gather near the dock for the speedboat to return to the island.

When my friend arrived, Gilda planned trips and we were taken for long rides on the Big Cruiser, named "B.G.". One place we stopped was a huge beautiful sandy beach. I remember walking out into the clear water and all of a sudden going under water. Seems I walked into some kind of hole under the water. I gasped for air and something to hold on to and just kept walking. I don't know how I got myself under control, but I did something right because I did not drown. No one seemed to notice anyway!

The water had some kind of creatures that would stick to your skin and then begin to hurt because they would suck out your blood. "Bloodsuckers" One stuck on me and I pulled it off. Then, my brother began to cry and one had gotten on him. That ended that trip. We returned to the Cruiser and had lunch and shortly went back to the island. No more playing in the water!

My friends and I would take hikes to the Teepee on the upper end of the island and wondered if Indians had ever lived there. While in the Tepee we would pretend it was a stage and we sang songs and pretended that the Indians had captured us and we were waiting to be saved.

On the way to the Teepee, there was a house that had since burned down and a statue of a young girl nearby. Later we learned the girl in the statue, was the daughter of Bror and his first wife Mary. The daughter would visit the island with her young child named Bonnie, within a few days. Then they sent Craig to camp on another island.

Another guesthouse with several differently decorated bedrooms is where we stayed. One of the rooms was decorated in an oriental black motif and very ornate. We decided that the woman had designed that room because it was dark and exotic and very mysterious. We would tell spook stories and conjure up murder stories that involved that room.

On our hikes we would see many kinds of rocks and stones. There were quartz rocks with gold flakes in them and we would make up stories of treasures and adventure and pretend they were real gold.

In the big house was a room, probably like a den. It was round with seats all around the outside perimeter; a bear rug and a large piano with a big fireplace graced the center. I learned later that this was where they had their parties and famous celebrities would come. The ceiling was designed much like the teepee and had some kind of pipe at the top. Later I learned this was for the smoke to escape from the huge fireplace.

MEALS

Each day we had a schedule for meals. If we missed it, there was no one there to give us anything to eat, so we would be sure to watch the time for dinner with care. The meals were full of variety and we had plenty of food at mealtime. Snacks were not available. They served very different foods from what I was accustomed to eating at home. Some had a very unusual flavor that we just did not like. We were taught to be gracious guests when invited somewhere for a meal so naturally no comments were made by me.

At home we had never eaten uncooked spinach or endive in salads. I could see that she would pamper Craig's wishes and sometimes get him what he wanted so he would try to eat the many different foods set before him.

I recall feeling a bit strange about the eating arrangements. My friends and I were instructed to eat in the servants' quarters in the kitchen.

(Now, my conclusion is this: Gilda wanted to create an atmosphere where family and familiar people were no longer a part of Craig's life. The more separation would help him to not miss us when we no longer were in his life. The lady wanted a boy child and my uncle was not enough for her.)

There was only one time she indicated an interest in me when I was alone between guests. She took me down by the boathouse and showed me a rickety bridge to get on a path to go across to the other side of the island. She encouraged me to go there and take long walks. I wondered if she just wanted me to disappear somewhere permanently. I did venture over but I saw some kind of larger animal (probably a bear) in the bushes. It scared me and I ran back to the path and across the familiar rickety bridge to what I thought was safety.

THE NUDE SUNBATHER

One day I was taking a walk and there was Gilda, bare-naked lying on the pier. I could hardly believe my eyes! I had never even seen anyone in my own family in the nude and here this lady was showing everything, even to people in the boats passing by. I was taught to be modest about myself and I certainly did not think adults should do this.

CAMPING ON THE OTHER SIDE OF THE ISLAND AND HOME COOKED STEW

On one excursion, we piled in several small boats for a campout dinner. She brought things to make homemade soup. I remember my brother joking and saying she was making ‘s o a p’. Everyone was recruited to peel potatoes, vegetables and cut the meat and put it into the pot. Then, she added all kinds of seasonings, catsup and sauces. With the preparation came words of intimidation that “this soup will be so delicious” the best you ever had!

Actually the brew actually tasted like poison and my brother made a horrible face, and said, “This tastes like poison.” It was awful and I wondered what trouble my brother might be in for saying what he did! I remember the expressions on everyone’s faces present so I don’t think anyone felt it was good at all. It amazed me that she did not get mad and start yelling at my brother, like she did most everyone else. At least she said nothing in our presence. She poured the soup on the ground and looked a bit angry but didn’t yell and scream like I had seen her do to the servants before. Even so, her very presence was intimidating, because she was so expressive and explosive at times. Almost like a spoiled child wanting her way.

We did have a wonderful time that summer, a summer I will always remember. But the summer did end and I went home to our parents. Again, my brother did not return home with me and I wondered why. I blamed myself for years for leaving him alone. No explanation was given and I dared not ask. I could sense the tenseness and the emotion that were always a part of our lives.

(Mother and Dad were always very quiet people and if they had any serious conversation it was done out of our ear range. If they ever

had a disagreement it was never obvious to me. I am sure today, that the next few months were sheer hell for my Mother when her son was not with her. What it did to her life was certainly evidenced by the years that followed.

My friend and I were sent home on the bus and the woman flew to California with my brother...**she "kidnapped" him again!** Taking him without my parents consent...It was now supposedly a "big misunderstanding". That is what she always claimed! That was what it was when she slapped a servant in the face years before and it was in the newspapers in Los Angeles. Our parents wrote letters, made telephone calls requesting them to return my brother to them. One excuse after another with news he has gone to camp, he is ill again, school has started and they should not disturb his school year. Whatever she could do to keep him in California with her at any cost. She took him to doctors and claimed he was unbalanced and blamed it on my parents. Of course he was a very troubled child and she was the cause.

VALET BRINGS CRAIG HOME

It was 1947 and the Dahlbergs Valet brought my brother home. We began to enjoy a somewhat normal life again. Mother asked me to be sure to help her watch over Craig no matter where we were. Everyone assumed that things were going to revert back to the way they had been prior to Craig's was having been taken from us. We would be normal, peaceful and quiet family again doing our usual family things like visiting our grandparents, building snowmen in the winter and swinging on grandparents swings in the summer.

Summer came and we stayed close to home. Dad did not make a lot of money as a postman so we did not take vacations but we did spend more time at both of our grandparents and we really enjoyed doing that. Craig was never allowed to play in the front yard alone. I would go with my friends and he would stay home with Mother and play with his cars and color in his coloring books. Sometimes he would bang on the piano.

Craig was a very quiet and content little boy while he was home with our little family. In the morning for breakfast, we both loved cinnamon toast and hot chocolate and we would see who could eat the most. Lunchtime Craig especially just loved peanut butter and jelly sandwiches. After lunch he enjoyed bringing his cars out on the kitchen floor and seeing how far he could make them scoot across the floor. Other times Mother would take time playing little games with him or teaching him songs. At one time he was interested in little magic tricks and tried making up some of his own.

FAMOUS VISITORS AND PHONE CALLS

The constant harassment began. The months came and went, but the phone never stopped ringing. Airmail letters and telegrams arrived regularly and finally some very prominent visitors came to our door. A famous Los Angeles paternal attorney (Joseph Scott) and an actor of a movie who portrayed the main character of a famous comic strip "Dagwood and Blondie" (Arthur Lake) came. He was a friendly sort of person and Craig and I were overjoyed and asked for his autograph. My cute brother,

Mr. Perfect (Craig) himself commented that on one word that didn't look right. He said, "It looked more like 'sappy' than happy! Mr. Lake corrected it by putting an "H" above the word. Everyone got a good laugh out of that one.

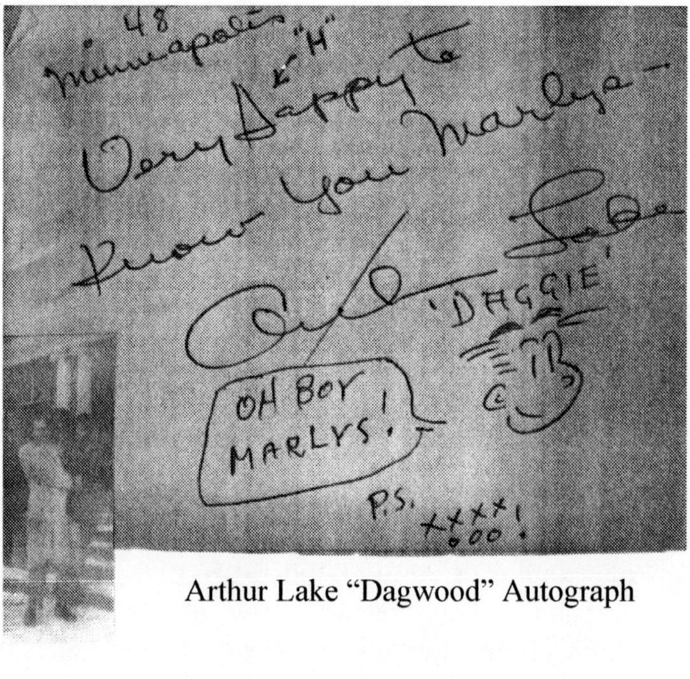

Arthur Lake "Dagwood" Autograph

Arthur Lake and Cousin Penny

Then, they tried to convince my parents into surrendering their darling blond boy to these wealthy people. They exclaimed, "After all they had no children, they could give him a good education, lovely home, —-just everything anyone would ever want! They insinuated he is so puny and so thin looking and made accusations of poor health and improper care." They continued to pressure them into giving into the Dahlberg's wishes.

My parents wanted their son home with them—after all, Craig was *their* son! It was absurd that people could just take away anyone's child and get away with it. But it certainly did happen to our family.

The wealthy couple and their helpers contacted both of my grandparent's ministers and made it sound as though my parents were not taking care of my brother properly. They later claimed to have their support and lied in their legal papers about many things. The famous Hollywood paternal attorney, Joseph Scott was the Dahlberg's attorney. In an attempt to scare my parents, he made a special visit to our home. The Mayor of Minneapolis was contacted. They contacted the newspapers and had articles written in their favor. They even tried to get my father fired from the Post Office and *contacted* other neighbors and friends to put on the pressure. It was both humiliating and embarrassing for my parents.

The harassment went on and on in various ways for months and months and they attempted in numerous ways to breakdown my parents resistance.

THE DAHLBERG'S SEND MY UNCLE HOME TO MAKE THEIR APPEAL with A LITTLE FRIEND

It was unusual and there was a lot of talking going on in the kitchen in the middle of the night. I was surprised when I got up and looked into our kitchen where my Uncle Milton, my parents and a very small person, whom later I learned was a dwarf and an actor. (Billy Barty) I wanted to go and greet my uncle but when my parents saw me they motioned that I should go back to bed.

I overheard a few words and I deducted that they were trying to convince my parents that they should take advantage of the generous offer of these wealthy people and allow them to adopt Craig. I recall them saying Craig was skinny, sick and mal-adjusted. Even as a child that certainly was not evident to me as long as he was home with us. They told them that Craig would get the best care money could buy, best education, medical expenses, meet the crème of society and become a man of whom one day they would be proud. Of course, they left out that along with all this would come total alienation from his natural parents and the loving care they had always provided to us children. (*Convinced by the Dahlbergs all this would be true, they may have not realized it's ultimate outcome.)*

Years later I questioned why my uncle was going along with this scheme and a well-rehearsed presentation. He enjoyed being in the spotlight, the exciting life he led living with them and the interesting people that he met. It wasn't stimulating for him to in a small town in Minnesota or work some menial job. These people enjoyed using him to entertain their guests and he enjoyed all they provided for him.

PART IV

WHAT KIND OF PEOPLE WERE OUR PARENTS?

How this could have even happened to them is still somewhat a mystery to me. From my prospective, they did not deserve any of what occurred in their lives. However, it did happen and one thing I learned from it is that "You have to learn to bounce with life's bad times as well as its blessings, but you certainly do not allow other's to take away your call to live life."

Yes, it is hard to understand how any person could forgive the repeated actions of another as shared in this story. Could it be that because Jesus Spirit lived in the hearts of both my parents they were able to forgive "Seventy times Seven"? The measure God himself places on the value of forgiveness.

It is still hard for me to totally accept or even understand because my brother was personally involved and taken without consent from our home. They were both loving and caring people who loved their children, their home and their family. Both my parents were very loving, sensitive, somewhat naive and fearful people. When the courts and judges ruled against them it broke their spirit because they sincerely believed in justice and the court system.

My father was a man of loyalty and integrity. I deeply respected and held him in high regard all of my life. I observed that friends and co-workers also held him in high regard because his word was as gold. "Pure and honest". If he said something you could count on him to carry through and do it. He was the head of our home probably because Mother esteemed him in our eyes. He wasn't perfect but he was a man with a subtle strength that made you feel secure and safe. His family was deeply loved and we never went hungry because he was conscientious about work and providing for us.

Mother was fragile, sensitive and passive, yet at times courageous. Some of that was passed on to all of their children. Mother was a person who easily yielded to the person in control with a more powerful personality. Yet, there were times she was able to go beyond self and conjure up courage when it came to the welfare of her children. In our eyes she earned our respect and the right to be called "M O T H E R".

The times she exhibited qualities that were beyond self, she was able to accomplish what I felt were miracles. Her fears and timidity turned into exceptional courage and strength when it came to her children. She was able to put aside that part of herself to accomplish what needed to be done. Mother had an inner strength I believe came from her personal relationship with the Lord. She prayed regularly but did not discuss her faith with anyone until the later years in life. It was a "private" thing for people of her age and church affiliation. Later in life her faith blossomed, as she was able to express her love for Him in various ways as she served helping in Vacation Bible School & the Convalescing Home.

Both of our parents attended church all of their early childhood years but they were of different protestant denominations. Because of that difference, for years they only attended church on the two significant holidays. When my little sister was about ten (10) years of age, that changed when she began going to church. Eventually our Dad became very involved in serving on the building committee for their church in Monterey Park, California.

(I loved my parents deeply and they loved me. My whole life I attempted to bring them some kind of happiness in whatever way and whenever I could. I tried to be an especially good and obedient child. I showered them with gifts and as many good things as I was able to give … trying to fix the hurt I knew existed in their lives. Today, they are together and what they once saw through a clouded glass, now they clearly see and fully know. I feel sure they completely forgive as well!)

MOTHER SHARES HER FAITH

Early in my childhood development, Mother was the one who taught me the "Lord's Prayer" and other prayers and spoke to me about God. I learned early in my childhood and my upbringing the basic principles of the Word of God, but I was never told that they were in the Bible. I was never pointed to Jesus Christ, except those two times a year when we would recall Jesus birth or death and go to church. That was Easter and Christmas.

(Later in my own life when I accepted Christ as my Savior, I remember hearing the story in the Old Testament about the two women who were fighting over a child, saying it was theirs. I related this to our story about my brother.

(I Kings 3:25) The judge said, "Let's just cut the child in half then" It was the real mother who said, "No, let her have him." She did not want her son cut in half or destroyed. I relate that story because that is what I believe the decision my parents made. Not having their son torn apart and destroyed in his spirit.

Mother and Dad wanted Craig to become all he could. That was their ultimate hope and purpose for deciding the way they did to stop fighting.

The *Old Testament story relates that the one who gave up the child was the one who truly loved the child. I know with all my heart my parents loved each one of their children as much as any parent could. Every man desires to raise his own son.)*

God sacrificed His only Son and sent Him to earth so we might also find life and become all we could. Maybe Daddy believed he was giving his son great opportunities to become somebody and do something good for the world. I know that he instilled for us girls to be good and do as much good for others as we could in our lives. The "Golden Rule" was often quoted to us in our home.

PROMISES...PROMISES.

The constant harassment and visitors, letters, telegrams, telephone calls and now promises of future happiness and reconciliation finally broke down my parents resistance. They finally agreed to move to California to be near my brother. Craig would continue to be enrolled in the best private school in Rolling Hills. (*Gilda enrolled my brother as her son with their last name, not with his legal given name.* (Doesn't this indicate what her intention was for a long time?) Court papers read that my parents could visit him on weekends and have him come home during the summer months.

Dad was promised a lifetime position with Celotex Corporation and was trained in Chicago. This was the product the man actually invented and the company that the wealthy Dahlberg started and owned. Mother, who never drove a car in her life, was to be given a brand new Chevrolet for Dad to drive to be able to handle this fantastic new lifetime job. They would pay for our furniture (meager as it was) to be moved to California and would pay the train fares for all of us. Mom, Cheryl and I were to go by train. Dad would drive with my aunt Marion and uncle Gus, who also will move to California and they would bring a trailer load of things.

My parents had paid premiums and surrendered Craig's Annuity Policy to the Dahlbergs in good faith. It was all they had to give them, but it was never mentioned again. They promised Craig would receive the medical care he needed and the Dahlbergs wanted to pay for it all, as well as a good education.

THE BIG MOVE TO BE NEAR CRAIG

The day arrived and finally Mother, Cheryl, Craig and I were off to California. We took a plane to Chicago where we were picked up by someone and taken for a nights stay in the Dahlbergs hotel suite overlooking Lake Michigan. While there, we took a walk along the beach to kill time. The cold wind whirled around our heads and water on the lake was rough. With the fall months approaching the wind was too cold and we decided to return to the hotel. There was a strange aroma in the apartment that smelled like Gilda and I did not like it.

In the morning we went to the train depot to begin our trip to California. We had our own private travel compartment and bath and we really got to know the conductor on the train, unlike the average traveler. They would bring our food to us in the little compartment at mealtimes and prepare the beds in the evenings. This was luxury only afforded those who had money, something we were not accustomed to enjoy.

WE ARE MET AT THE TRAIN IN PASADENA

I looked out of the window of the train as the passengers were getting off and to my delight, I recognized Betty Hutton and Fred Briskin. They were just married! Reporters from the news media with cameras and bulbs flashing were all over the train station. I wanted to go and get their autograph because she was one of my favorite actresses but Mother said that I shouldn't bother her on her wedding day.

Gilda with her chauffer and limousine picked us up at the train and took us to her home for a couple days. We thought we would be staying with her until Daddy arrived.

"YOU ARE GOING TO A MOTEL"

I could see that Mother was surprised when Gilda announced that Mother, Cheryl and I would be taken to a motel to wait Dad's arrival. We were *not* taken to a nearby motel in Beverly Hills or San Fernando Valley but taken twenty-five miles away to the San Gabriel Valley, which rather left us stranded.

We were taken to a Motel on Colorado Boulevard in Pasadena. (This is the route of the annual New Years Day "Rose Parade".) We just had to sit and await the arrival of Daddy, Aunt Marion and Uncle Gus who were driving out from Minnesota with a trailer full of our things.

They were late arriving and two days we ran out of money for food to eat. My Mother went without food a day or two before to be sure us kids had something. I recall mother buying one hamburger each day and sharing it between my sister and I. Every time we said we were hungry, she would have us drink water. It seemed to help some but we didn't really understand why we couldn't have any food.

The Motel lady gave us a grapefruit and even though I did not like it, being famished it tasted good! Mother would keep us busy taking walks, coloring, telling stories to us, and listening to music on the radio, whatever seemed to work to help the daylight hours pass by.

Mother must have been worried but she never let on. I realized we did not have any money and she didn't know what to do but wait for Dad. Those days we did not have cell phones to call one another. Since we did not have any money either, all we could do was wait. Bless Mother for her courage and inner strength to be with two young children who were so hungry and not have money to purchase anything at all. Mother had a lot of pride and she would not beg or tell anyone about our situation. She would not call the wealthy lady who put us in this situation. She had not expected this to happen and just reminded us that Daddy would be here anytime! Waiting was a hard thing to do when the stomach is talking to you! When I hear of children starving throughout the world today, I remember that one day I was hungry too.

Finally Dad arrived and we went out for Chinese food. We were so hungry. (*If one has ever been truly without food, I am sure appreciation for eating becomes rather significant. I always hope I can help someone from never having to go hungry.*)

Uncle Milt in front of our Rented Home in Alhambra, Ca

OUR NEW HOME

We set out right away to find a house to rent because the Motel cost was just too much. We found a house in Alhambra and my aunt and uncle found one just in back of us on the next street. Dad bought a new mattress and we all slept on the floor with our clothes for warmth. The furniture was to arrive in a big moving van. It was late too, and it was cold weather for California but we all survived. We were together and togetherness is always warm!!

Within days I was registered in school in the seventh grade. Everything was somewhat quiet. Gilda never came to our house and fewer phone calls were received. Craig was in the private school and for some reason, never came to our home even though I understood that was their agreement.

VISITS TO BEVERLY HILLS HOME

I do remember a few visits to their home in Beverly Hills. One time her nephew was playing the piano. He was accomplished and I really enjoyed his music. He is now a very successful musician in the entertainment industry. (Out of respect I omit his name) His mother was a very nice person and was there also.

Another time, I remember my little sister falling into the swimming pool and my brother jumped in and saved her. On one of the visits we were playing in the pool and I was trying to learn how to swim using an air filled preserver and trying to take it off and swim without it. But I never learned to swim.

One visit was when our grandparents Johnsen were here from Minnesota. Bror seemed very interested in talking to my grandfather while Dad helped Craig learn to ride a bike. Grandmother, Mother and I must have been visiting with Gilda or just sitting around. I believe she served us some kind of refreshments also.

Craig
and His Collie (top)

Grandpa J. – Craig – Dad   Grandma J – Craig – Cheryl - Mother

VISITS TO MY BROTHERS SCHOOL

Daddy made a visit to see my brother in the private school. They said he was not registered there and then, he learned that Gilda had registered him in their last name—Dahlberg. He advised the school that he was not registered correctly and attempted to explain the situation.

We had to travel to Rolling Hills (Pacific Palisades) from Alhambra to visit him every Sunday afternoon.. This was before there were freeways and going and coming took most of the day, with only a couple hours to visit and play with him. Dad used to play ball with him while my mother, sister and I watched.

When I was about fifteen years old and beginning to date a boy. I stopped going to see my brother but my parents remained faithful to visit regularly every week. While Craig was at Chadwick Private School our grandparents Johnsen came out for a visit and they took a few pictures.

SCHOOL SEASON ENDS AT PRIVATE SCHOOL

On a weekend at the end of the school semester, Dad drove to the Rolling Hills Private School and picked up my brother and brought him home to be with us. This was after the second summer he was at the school, the first summer he never did come home to be with us as promised.

When Gilda found out about it she obtained some kind of court order against my parents and sent a policeman with the papers to pick my brother up. He was only with us a few hours. We were so happy being together. We took lots of pictures of each other. My boyfriend came over. Craig didn't seem to like my boyfriend. Probably no real reason except he was the reason I no longer visited him at school.

The police officer came to our door and served papers on my parents. When they told Craig he would have to go to Gilda's house with the policeman, Craig objected. He sat <u>defiantly pleading not to be sent back.</u> I remember the agony in his eyes. I remember him saying very defiantly, "I don't want to go, and I am not going." He was protesting with all he had in him and did not want to go to the Dahlberg's home ever again. Our parent's eyes told me they felt helpless against the law. Surprised again but the intrusion into our lives, they didn't think to call an attorney.

Our Family
Mother, Dad, Marlys, Craig and Cheryl
Last time we were together as a family.

Our parents, trapped by the law, had to tell him that they had to abide by the laws and those papers left them no alternative. If they did not let him go back they could end up in jail. Again this obsessed woman named Gilda had caused an event that traumatized our family and especially a dear young boy who needed his parent's love and care. He had to go with the policeman to her house once again.

When things are too much in our family, we all become silent. Tears flowed from our Mother's eyes as she cared for my younger sister. During the rest of the day our home was extremely quiet as each dealt with the trauma of the day. Dad sat with his head bowed down so we could not see the tears in his eyes. He probably questioned the law and how it could inflict such harm on a law-biding citizen by taking his son away. Both of my parents felt helpless to keep and to even help the son they dearly loved. What was Craig going through once again as he was taken by a policeman? Taken to a place he actually expressed that he hated to go.

He probably felt betrayed by my parents and never did understand how so much power was given to someone who was not his family. Possibly all the elements of feeling rejected filled his emotions. Undoubtedly, once again the events of the day caused by this malicious, selfish, covetous and thoughtless woman would cause Craig mental and emotional harm that would cripple his adult decisions and emotions to become complete and whole human being. Exactly the opposite of what my parents had desired for their young son. They were helpless to change the course of his life, their God-given right to do if at all possible.

After they drove off, I looked at Dad and I saw a tear in his eye. He just sat in his chair looking at the paper. I doubted if he was really reading it. I could tell his emotions were getting the best of him and thinking what can I do? Our family traumatized again! All of our hearts were in pain again, each one of us dealing with it the best we could. We just did not understand how the legal system could be on their side and do this to us.

It did not seem that our little family could ever be happy and let it last. Every time Gilda interfered with any happiness we found.

(I can only imagine what thoughts penetrated Craig's mind and the trauma again of his being torn from our home. What right did she have to just come and take him away? It was obvious that Craig

wanted to be home with us. I often wonder what his reaction was when he saw her. Was he passive and yielding or was he angry? How did any of us keep from losing our sanity? Mother and Dad's coping mechanism was always in check to keep us girls from being upset... inside I was upset also, but hid it as well!)

My parents contacted the attorney (Sam Yorty, former Mayor of Los Angeles) who helped my parents take my brother home from California. He was running for public office and could not take the case so he referred them to some one else. That attorney (*who shall remain nameless)* convinced them to sue the Dahlbergs, probably because that was one way he could get a nice fee. So they did. My parents did not own a home and what they did own was very modest and not worth very much.

Now, according to newspaper articles the Dahlbergs were giving false stories to the newspapers. Their version of the story looked as though all my parents were interested in was money for their son. A story, and lie from pit of hell. Yet, court papers filed for my parents by the attorney "actually object" to a sale of a human being. They were totally overlooked by the judge. Everyone distorted the truth, believing that was the real reason.

(It was unbelievable to my parents who held truth and honesty a high priority in their own lives and teaching us girls to hold in high priority. There was always a price to pay if you went against the wishes of this woman and they paid it! They paid the highest price any parent could pay.....the life of their son!

(Could it have been possible that she knew something we were never really allowed to learn and that was "just how very deeply my brother loved his parents and cared for his family and wanted to be with us?"

It remains a mystery why for so many years Gilda was so rentless in her efforts and continuously went to such extreme measures to keep us apart... when it was our family who held his heart.

Our conclusion has been that she had an "abnormal sick obsession" about him, possessing his very being and life, trying to make people believe he was her son. In his own way, he sabotaged her efforts and prolonged its eventual end by not *signing his own adoption papers until he was twenty-eight years old. Then, he finally succumbed to it the same way my parents did, which was accepting the inevitable!!! He succumbed to an unending battle he believed he could not win!!*

Human beings have no right to hold another in 'bondage' and curtail their natural and normal development. Not even parents! This kind of love is sick and it makes everyone who is a part of it—sick in one way or another! Even the birds and the animal's let their young go, teaching them to be independent creatures able to care for themselves and their new family.

My brother never learned some basic's about living, yet, had everything materially.

This continuous trauma and confusion under which my brother learned to exist was so unnecessary. That little thing called "good genes" and an early loving family, he did remember, kept him going in spite of what happened in his life. And I am sure that loving prayers of our Mother and Father were there as well.

Days before my brother died, he asked me this question. "Why did Gilda have to take me out of the family? Why couldn't she have adopted a child that didn't have a family? I couldn't answer his question. Now, in eternity, he has his answer and knows all truth!)

DAD'S PROMISED LIFE TIME JOB VANISHES —— HE IS TERMINATED! *(Possible punishment for bringing Craig home for a day!)*

After we had gotten a rental to live in, Dad left for ten days for training in Chicago with Celotex Corporation. He returned and went to work in Los Angeles. After only a month or so, he was notified that he was being 'terminated' due to "reduction of the forces". Now, where was the man who owned the company who hired him and promised him a lifetime job with a bright future? The promised reconciliation with his son here in California where Dad was convinced it would be better for Craig's health and education. We would have regular visits with him.

Now, the Dahlbergs that had proclaimed and were so compassionate and concerned about the welfare of this darling little boy had caused our family of five incredible pain and hardships. Dad was very disappointed and disillusioned. Instead of mopping around he just got out and began hunting for another job. He had a wife and three children to care for so he didn't have much time to get depressed about what had just happened to his future. Everyday he went out and looked for a job in the roofing construction field, hoping that the training he had at the Chicago Celotex office would be adequate to get one.

Finally, he met Charlie Gilstrom of O.K. Roofing in Los Angeles. He was willing to pay him a weekly salary until he learned the business. The only catch was that Dad agreed to pay him back the borrowed money as soon as he was making some money.. He worked for Charlie until Charlie died. He paid back every dime and was well respected for doing it, even by his son Harry who took over the business.

This arrangement would at least pay the rent and feed his family. But times were still lean for our little family and it took years for him to pay the money back. We had nothing extra for vacations or even clothes. Dad agreed and did exactly what he promised, but it was a tremendous sacrifice and struggle for our family.

He was determined to become the best in his field of commercial roof estimators. And that is exactly what he did! Later he even passed the contractors test and allowed someone else with finances to use the license and he worked for him. Many of his accounts would not allow anyone else to do the take-offs or even give bids because Dad was so well respected and liked.

(In my young mind I had already figured out that there was "not a tiny bit of compassion" in these peoples hearts for our little family. They were going to "take" my brother away one way or another. They left a whole family without money or even a job. They lied and the newspapers, the law and the judges all believed them. As a child, I just did not understand that kind of justice. I still don't! They moved us to California and away from everything familiar and safe to us and then, practically left us destitute.

My parents were independent and proud people and they did not tell their own parents all that was taking place, especially that they were left destitute at one point.

And the Newspaper articles said that what they were doing was "out of the goodness of their hearts?"...Newspapers had no clue to what the truth really was and they sided with the Dahlberg's because they gave them the story and enjoyed the notoriety)

Later when the Dahlbergs filed legal papers again against my parents, they listed all of the above items, expenses and promises as payment for them to be able to continue to be an influential part of my brother's life. Insinuating in legal papers that my parents had "sold" my brother to them. Every part of the agreement they broke and violated, moving so far away to Florida my parents could no longer see and visit him. (Taking him out of the State of California without my parents consent or knowledge the day they were to go to court in Los Angeles and Craig age 14 was to decide where and whom " he wanted to live with" in front of a Judge. Craig may have answered that question posed to him by Gilda in a manner that was not pleasing to her. This may have caused her to skip the court hearing and take him to Florida. (Note: Later, when he was 18 and drafted in the training in Fort Jackson, I was able to find him again. When Gilda found out, she got him out of the army and took him further away to Europe. I have a letter in my files to this affect!)

AMIDST ALL THIS WE TRY TO LIVE NORMALLY

When sis was around four or five years old she was given dance lessons up town and she even tried out for the Disney Mouseketeers. Cheryl loved dancing and music and was a very active child. Two girls, born eleven years apart both very different, one an introvert and the other a born extrovert. She was so cute and everyone adored her.

FATHER MAKES DINNER ...Enjoy a little laugh with me!

Every Friday night, mother would take my sister Cheryl to town for a dancing lesson. Before she left she would usually prepare something for us that Dad could reheat. On this particular night she had prepared some waffle batter and had left Dad complete instructions reading, "Please plug in socket and let the iron heat until the arrow is to the left of the red mark." This red mark indicated that the iron was then 'too hot' and it was the time to pour in the batter.

When Dad arrived home he carefully glanced at the note. Proceeding to prepare the meal for that night, he carefully let the arrow go to the right of the red mark and poured the mixture into the iron. Poof!! The way he tells it... A black cloud of smoke blew up in the air; the batter was burnt to pieces! After trying to clean up the mess, he became discouraged and decided to try something different! "Fried waffles"

When Mother arrived home, her eyes glanced first at the mess on the table and then to the greasy, hard and hideous looking object in the frying pan. It is hard to even imagine what a man will do when he is hungry. Needless to say this was truly one of the funniest sights I remember as a teenager. Amazing what a man will do when he is desperate for food.

Mother's inner-pain was constant and it seemed that her thoughts about my brother subsided when she had little Cheryl who kept her so busy. Cheryl was a beautiful child and bright and challenging with her inquisitive spirit. Once she learned to talk, it seemed she never stopped. As I look back now, I think God had a special plan in sending us this new child into our home. She probably saved my mother's sanity! Yet, Mother (and Dad too) never forgot their little boy. Mother would write him letters every week when we had an address she would mail them…and some were returned unopened.

Mother loved to express herself by writing poems about life and the beauty that she saw through her eyes. During her lifetime she wrote several and one Christmas we made a little booklet and she gave them to all her friends to enjoy.

On one occasion when she was thinking and probably praying for my brother, she wrote the following poem, which speaks of a Mother's longing for her child. Mother was a magnificent human being and Craig was cheated of enjoying the life she gave to her children.

MY WISH
By Mildred Johnsen

As the days go by I wish I'd hear,
The doorbell ring loud and clear.
That standing there so big and tall,
My boy I haven't seen for many a fall.

His smile so radiant and divine,
His laughter, so hearty and sublime.
These memories I keep in my heart,

Ever since the day we've been apart.

For this wish each day to God I pray,
And I know He will grant it in His way.
A grand and glorious day twill be,
When my darling son, Craig, I see.

At first Mother and Dad would send gifts to Craig, but they never received one acknowledgement that Craig had received them. Then, they decided to sending checks or a few dollars cash, hoping he would get them. Our grandparents would also send Craig cards and money; and they never received any thank you or acknowledgement either. Of course he was a child, but Gilda was careful not to put such things in writing to be needed later as "proof" that my parents did not abandon my brother.

(*The emotional harm of these events took their toll on my Mother's and Dad's life and spirit. Most of her years, Mother was extremely nervous and stressful. Midst her suffering she did her best to raise my sister and I without having her own stress spill over into our lives. Not until just before she died, did she ever know the scar it held for me. Dad held hatred in his heart for his personal pain caused by Gilda. His hatred he hid well from all his family and friends. And of course, only in part what a lasting affect it held for my brother being taken away from his natural parents and living with this strange and domineering woman, who stripped him from his own family ties).*

PART V

Legal Fight Begins ... False accusations made!

COURT ACTION

In December a set of Legal Documents announcing that the couple wanted Legal Guardianship of my brother arrived at our home. A court date was stated and my brother would be present to make a statement.

The night before we were to go to Court in Los Angeles, I had a most unusual dream that I have never forgotten. I attempted to tell my parents but they scoffed off what I was trying to tell them. The dream only came in strong words and they were "Don't trust the attorney."

(*Now that I am older, I wonder if he sold them out. Many years after this event when I was married, I telephoned him. He was cold and indifferent and I felt his attitude was cold towards me for no reason. The conversation was abrupt as though I were pricking his conscience a bit. What could I do? I was only seeking information as a grown adult about what had taken place. I had no proof of anything and years had gone by. Didn't he remember what really happened? The comment he made was ... that my parents gave my brother away! The comment made me feel anger inside. I should have asked him more questions. I just said that was not true and bid him goodbye.)*

The prior guardian agreement stated when my brother turned fourteen years of age, he was to go to court and tell the judge ' where he wanted to live'. He was to decide at that time, which home he wanted to live—our family or the Dahlbergs. .... <u>The agreement was that everyone would abide by Craig's decision.</u>

(*My assumption now, from what took place...I believe that they knew his choice would be to go back and live with his birth family. And she could not allow that to take place.)*

Papers were filed and our family went to court fully expecting my brother to be there along with the wealthy couple. We waited and waited all day long for them to arrive and for the case to come before the judge.

Newspaper photographers were there and took our picture. (*copy enclosed in end of book)* I remember reading articles written, calling my brother, "an abandoned child", as though he was left on the street corner" That was far from the truth!.(*If anyone left him there Gilda did!)* It was never observed or written about the good care given to my sister and me or why would they abandon their son? Where did those news reporters get their stories? (*We knew!)* It was obvious, even to a child! Stories placing my parents in an unfavorable light, which were just plain lies. Daddy wasn't very cooperative with the reporters and was not willing to give them a story, so the stories they wrote only reflected one side of the case that was based on lies. (*This was probably not a wise decision but Dad was a very private kind of guy.)*

Finally Bror appeared with their attorney in court and he told the judge that his wife and my brother would not be in court. He never was asked to tell the reason they were not there. The case was postponed until another date. *(A date that never came about.)*

Shortly after the court hearing, my parents learned that she had taken my brother "out of their reach" again without their consent or knowledge off to Florida. (Kidnapped means taking a child without the parent's consent) I don't think they felt they could accuse her of that so didn't do anything about it. Everyone seemed to believe their lies and was on their side. My brother was again— unreachable and untouchable. Traumatized Again!!

The obsession this woman to possess my brother was without boundary. She would break the law and the law did nothing to her. My parents began to believe that they just could not fight the power she possessed because her influence and wealth.

They knew that my parents did not have the money to travel to Florida to get my brother or to 'fight' them and their influences. My parents did not even own their own home so had nothing to use as collateral to get a loan. Again they were miles away in California, from everything familiar and their son taken from them to another state.

Their hearts were broken and I am sure that the two of them shed many tears after they put my little sister and me to bed that evening. They said very little but I could feel the suffering and pain they endured. Mother always seemed very nervous. Agreements and promises meant nothing to these people and my parents felt totally helpless.

THE LAST PAGES INCLUDE

MISCELLANEOUS PAPERS AND NEWSPAPER CLIPPINGS

REFERRING TO THIS STORY PROVING ITS AUTHENTICITY.

—LOTS OF YEARS PASSED BY—.

DOES TIME HEAL?

My parents tried to make our new home in California as normal as possible for my sister and me. But our brother was the missing part I never could truly accept or forget. If my own pain felt like this, I could only imagine what it was for them to know that their son was alive, somewhere??? Mother and Dad dealt with it by talking very little about it to family or friends. Occasionally the subject would come up but they were very reserved about any information they shared. In spite of their own personal pain, they decided to accept what they could not change and just live with it.

NO PERSONAL CONTACT

The way my mother would try to keep her sanity was by writing letters to my brother, sending them return receipt and wonder if he ever got one of them. All they had was an attorney's name and address and the Celotex address which they had been previously advised to NOT write and send packages through their offices in Los Angeles.

(*It was evident that this wealthy woman wanted to "cut away" any relationship that my brother had with his family and remove any happy memories from his mind. Adults have a way of underestimating the memory of a child. All memories are hidden deep in the memory banks of the brain. It is amazing to me that I remember so many details of what occurred as I write this story.)*

For years there was no contact with Gilda or Bror. We did not have a direct address we could write to, no way to make any personal contact by telephone, no telephone number we could call and talk to him, and know that my brother received our letters, cards or gifts.. (*Just to hear their son's voice might have helped relieve their suffering! Gilda forbade any contact at all. She stole away my parents rights.)*

My parents tried to secure some help from the Red Cross and Social Services but there was no advice or help available. The attorney said he could do nothing. There was absolutely no one to help anywhere to find a missing child. It might have been possible if you had lots of money to pay an investigator or money to find them yourself. My parents were already financially burdened. *We had no luxuries, low paying job and didn't own but very little furniture and clothing.*

Parents who merely wanted the best for their son, and it now appeared to have sold him. Unbelievable—and certainly *not true*.

Rather than keeping my brother's life in a constant turmoil and confusion, parents decide to pray and just "wait" for him to become of age and return home. *Resigned to defeat, without any financial backing to support their cause, humbly they succumb to the inevitable.*

TOO BIG A BATTLE

This battle was way above my parents' heads. One that appeared they would lose. It seemed to them that they had no choice but to wait it out. Wait until my brother was 21 years old and just came home was their hope and dream.

They talked and thought about the lies they were sure that Gilda told him about being "abandoned" by them. Also, that they "sold" Craig to her. Even possibly telling stories that my parents didn't care about him or love him. Gilda claiming that that she loved and cared about him more than anyone.. He would never know about the hundreds of letters mother wrote or the little gifts of love sent to him.

All he could remember was about the times he wanted to stay at "home" and was "forced" to go with Gilda. He never knew how painful it was for his parents to always have to yield to the laws and the courts and how she could say and get away with just about anything.

The few times our parents exerted their legal rights, she became outraged and followed-up doing awful things like kidnapping him or taking him to a location out of my parents reach.

They never expected it would last indefinitely. Their son had the same genes and was unable to fight and win against the same foe as theirs. He was traumatized over the many incidents in his own life. They were helpless to protect him and take him away out of her grip because even the authorities were not supportive of their plight. Helpless against a ruthless foe!

Mother fell asleep many a night with my brother on her mind and in her heart. All she could do was pray. I am sure after years of prayer, she wondered if God heard her prayers and would ever answer! Mother had quiet amazing faith. She never made any comment against God in her total life, almost a sense of never questioning His plan or Sovernity. She taught us girls about a very loving and kind God.

Today I question whether it was total denial of the facts or merely self-preservation that caused Mother and Dad to always picture their son as getting a good education, being well-liked in school and becoming a well adjusted human being as long as he did not have to live in constant turmoil, being constantly bashed around between them and Gilda.

"Our parents had an uncanny way of believing "everything would turn out for the best" even under the most unhappy circumstances. They also had a way of "accepting their lot in life what-ever the amount of pain and suffering accompanied the trials they had to bear. (As you read the conclusion.. you will see even further how true this was of their lives.) By their example, these strong character traits have been passed on to us girls as a legacy of their own personal faith in God. Our parents deeply loved one another, giving us a deep sense of security.)

LIVING IN FLORIDA

There was a boy named Craig, now living in Florida with blond hair and blue eyes and was loved deeply by his own natural parents, sisters and family. In our hearts we always pictured a well-adjusted normal boy. But deep in our hearts we knew that whoever knew him, taught him, saw him really knew there was a "huge gap of deep hurt in his heart and life" that they could never reach or understand. And no one evidently ever tried!

Some wrongfully believe— if a person lives with wealth, they "have it made" and life is beautiful, they have no pain or problems! Craig a quiet-passive child never revealed his personal pain and probably merely accepted the inevitable—just like our parents.

Any child that is not allowed contact with his natural parents. Not a telephone call or a visit suffers immeasurable damage. Then, to add to Craig's pain were lies and false stories told about their parents. The liar believes the lies they have told which makes them convincing stories to the hearer. (*It would be interesting to read a psychiatrist evaluation of what happens to an individual who is deprived of the pure form of family love.)*

Why didn't our parents just fly there and take him home again? By now, they believed it was virtually impossible! The law and the courts had not favored them, even though he was their son. Not one judge questioned their having two other healthy normal children at home. They never had us "evaluated" to see if we were healthy or emotionally and psychologically stable! Everyone believed the lies they told about my brother being abandoned, that he was not taken care of properly and/or my parents "sold" him.

Our parents compared to "one of the richest men in America" were basically poor! They did not have credit cards, did not own a home and had very little credit which all goes along with being married young and having a young family. They were inexperienced to fight against such odds.

Somewhere along the trail of information we learned he was attending Graham Eckes School in Miami and was apparently a good student. (*I would be interested in hearing from anyone who knew my brother.)*

BROR DAHLBERG DIES

Just before the wealthy man died, the Dahlbergs had made out Legal Papers to adopt my brother mentioning in the papers that his own parents had "abandoned" him…a lie told again and again. A lie from the pit of hell, he was kidnapped/taken without their full consent from his parents!

Our parents responded that all they wanted to do was talk to their son and if that was his decision, they would honor it. But they wanted to be in his presence and talk to him personally. Mrs. Dahlberg refused to allow this, probably because she knew that he would never return to her and she couldn't take that chance. Nothing more happened!

MARLYS GRADUATES FROM HIGH SCHOOL AND GETS MARRIED

Graduating from high school was a meaningful milestone in my life. My grandparents Hultgren came to California for my graduation and I was so tickled to have them there. I had a job as a waitress and felt pretty good about myself. I still lived at home and was anxious to be on my own.

I had been writing to a sailor who seemed very special and through the letters I felt I had come to know him very well. He came home from the service and we dated and believed we were madly in love. Within two weeks we ran off and were married. A couple years passed and when I learned that Bror died, the memories come alive again of what these people have done to my family. Again I began a new search for my brother.

Grandparents Hultgren and Marlys

THRUST TO FIND BROTHER BEGINS.

I knew that when my brother turned eighteen he would have to register for the services. I wrote to our Armed Services Department and miraculously learned that my brother was in the service at Ft. Jackson, Florida.

I found the telephone number and called and was able to talk to him for a few minutes. I was so excited but I felt like I was on a mission greater than myself. My brother said, "Is that really you?" I told him that I loved him and that I would write him a letter. He said, "I love you too and give Mom and Dad my love." I promised I would deliver the message to them.

(When I heard his voice and I knew it was my brother, even after all those years.) I told him that we had been trying to find him for years. I told him that Mother and Dad would never sign the adoption papers because they wanted to see him and talk to him in person to know if that is what 'he wanted'. I told him that I would send a letter the next day. I wrote and reaffirmed what I said over the telephone. I also told him about the hurtful things Gilda had done, telling him as much as I could about everything in that letter.

Then a second letter I sent was returned to me. I then wrote to the base Chaplain and he wrote back to me. He wrote, " I pray you will be able to get in contact with your brother again*." (Today, I believe that Craig confronted her with the truth and she denied it, told him I was lying and I could not possibly remember what happened because I was a child.)* .

OUT OF REACH…THEY GO TO EUROPE

She wrote my parents how she had 'saved' my brothers life, just like she had saved my Uncles Milton's life by getting him out of the service. (*We still have these letters.)* She always said things hoping to get a favorable response of gratitude from my parents. They only had distain for her. When my parents told me about the letter, I reacted with a letter of response that I am sure she did not like. I wrote that we didn't think any of ourselves are better than others and we all should do our part and serve our country.

Gilda wrote to me and I wrote that we would plan a trip to visit my brother in about a year. I should never have written this because that really set her imagination on fire and she began her insidious plan to make it harder for us to go to him.

Shortly thereafter, she took my brother further away again. Gilda seemed to always panic and think that we would go and take him from her. This time she moves even further away to Europe. Certainly out of a determined sisters reach as well as her pocketbook..

ADOPTION PAPERS

Within months, the wealthy Gilda's nephew, who was an attorney in Florida, arrived unexpectedly at my parent's home with adoption papers. Asking them to sign the adoption papers once again for the benefit of my brother. My parents refused stating. "That on no terms would they ever sign adoption papers without personally speaking to Craig about what he wanted." They proceeded to recall the deliberate act performed before which denied them access to Craig when Gilda left the State of California taking Craig with her when he was to appear in court at age 14 to make his own decision in this matter. He explained that my brother could sign his own papers when he became of age. (*Interestingly enough: He never signed them until years later when he was 28 years old—-what did he have to lose?)* My parents tell him that they realize that they could do nothing about that and asked the attorney to leave their home.

My brother would never know the love my parents truly had for him. He would receive a broad education, travel and meet some very interesting people. He always had servants doing things for him. The wealthy woman made most if not all his decisions, handled the finances and separated him from everyone who might become an influence or a love in his life. (*Her obsession and possession with my brother in my opinion destroyed his spirit and his life. Not to mention how deeply it hurt and scarred my own parent's hearts and lives. (I will share more about that later.)*

Cards, gifts and letters to my brother must be sent through the Florida attorney who in turn would mail them to their address in Europe. An attorney in Europe would receive the mail. I never knew if my brother received the mail. He never responds, wrote or called.

Mother-Cheryl-Dad-Marlys

Marlys-Dad-Mother 1954

PART VI

Craig is somewhere in Europe ... I try to locate him
Marlys Remarriage and Auto Accident ...Correspondence Begins

MY SEARCH FOR MY BROTHER CONTINUES

My interest in getting in personal contact with my brother was rekindled. I began writing letters to the American Embassies all over Europe. I write the Census Bureau, Passport and Visa offices, Customs Office, the American Newspaper in Italy. My every idea was pursued with a letter of inquiry. Someone gave me a clipping from a Daily American newspaper in Rome and I wrote to them learning that my brother did work for them but he was gone now.

I received a telegram from someone in Italy requesting $3,000. I was advised not to send money there as it probably was not my brother who sent it even though it was supposedly, signed by him. Probably fortunate for us we did not have $3,000 to send or give to anyone. It all seemed very suspicious. If it was Craig I wanted to help him so I thought I could outsmart someone who was trying to embezzle the money from us and I had an idea. We sent a message that if the person would call us and answer a question on the telephone to us, we would send it. My question had to do with something only Craig would have remembered. When he was little I used to tease him by calling him a pet name. It was "Eggie" and it used to make him really angry with me. The telephone call never came and we never sent the money.

(Years later when I asked my brother he said, "I never requested any money from you at any time." So then, we knew it was hoax and someone else was trying to extort money from us.)

The London Embassy called him in and after that some communication was made. Gilda sent a letter along with one from my brother. She may have hopefully encouraged him to write so she wouldn't get in trouble with the immigration department believing she was some sort of criminal and make her leave the country

I looked at some of the old society clippings we had collected over the years to learn about people that they knew. I began to write everyone, everywhere like: Ginger Rogers mother, Mrs. Douglas Fairbanks Jr., May Mann, John Warburton, Mary Pickford, Alan Ladd, Jet-set Suzy Parker and other people I had met in their Beverly Hills Mansion.

WEDDING

It was 1960. I was planning to get married and sent off a letter to them at the attorney's address requesting their presence at our wedding. Gilda wrote me a very nice letter telling me all about what she wanted me to believe about my brother. She also said she really appreciated being invited to our wedding. I really didn't expect either of them to attend, but like Mother, I always had hope that things would change throughout the years. She sent us a check for $25.00. (*Other than the bathing suit, that was the only gift I ever received from this millionaire.)* Then a big surprise, she also gave me an address and telephone number where I might reach my brother by telephone. That was the biggest gift of all as far as I was concerned and something we had wanted for many years—-personal contact with him. My brother was supposed to be in Rome, Italy. I called many times without any success.

Her letters said that he was working on one of the European Newspapers and was a successful writer. We found copies of the "Daily American" and made contact with them to learn that he no longer worked for them.

The way she always did things, it made me think it probably was just a vacant apartment she rented to throw us off course again! I wrote back telling her I couldn't reach them and she wrote back that Craig had left and disappeared. Something, we learned later was evidently a customary pattern for him when things got too much for him to cope..

AUTO ACCIDENT

Six months after we were married, I was in an auto accident and had a whip lash and I cut my arm pretty bad. I had to have six months of heat therapy on my neck to relieve the headaches. I hoped this would stir my brother's emotions and he would rush to be by my side. I really expected a miracle!

Instead a letter came from her that she had not heard from my brother in three months. I just did not believe that because she wouldn't let him out of her sight. She said that she had been in the movie "Roar of a Dove". She said that she had married an Italian by the name of Rota, so she could work in Italy. She said it was a marriage of convenience, not love!

Another letter arrives, my brother had disappeared and she did not know where he was. Her letter sounded frantic…possibly she thought he had come home!

I wrote to the American Embassy in several countries. Within two weeks Craig wrote back. "Please don't do that anymore because it gets me into trouble. . etc." At last something — finally personal a word from Craig. I was overjoyed to at last see his own handwriting and have something tangible to hang on to… giving me H O P E for the future. He finally knows I care and was still looking for him. I hoped it would make a difference to him that someone was still thinking of him.

The end of that year she wrote that my brother had a girlfriend and they were taking ski trips and he would not be home for Christmas.

Almost a year went by and I wrote the attorney in Florida. He wrote back that he could do nothing. Of course I understood his family loyalty and respected him for it.

Six months later, I wrote him again and he stated that he wished he could help, but couldn't. *(Later you will learn the important role he played in a happier ending after she was dead.)*

The month of May arrived and I received a letter that my brother's relationship with the young lady had broken off and that he was in the hospital 'heartbroken' over the love affair. She is careful to never give any information that we could check up on and make a personal contact with Craig. We have no idea of the name of the hospital or the girlfriend— and /or we could not go to his side or help.

Just like with our family, *it is my opinion that* Gilda probably interfered with the relationship because they were getting serious. By this time, my parents were better off financially and would have flown to his side, but we had absolutely no information available to us. If I asked such a question, it was always left unanswered.

At least Gilda was writing me more often and I welcomed any news. True, false or indifferent. When I wrote to her I tried using every technique I knew to manipulate her into doing something that would enable us to have personal contact with my brother. It didn't work! Unfortunately she was probably smarter than I; after all she was twice my age plus some. No matter what she said, I knew I couldn't really believe it and took it as a grain of salt and her words had no affect at all. But I kept writing, with the 'hope in my heart' that one day it would pay off!!

At the end of the year, I tried again to spark the attorney's heart. No response. Two years later I humbled myself and asked Gilda for tickets to go see my brother. No response. She now knew travel for me would be a financial burden. I was no treat to her.

Now I tried writing more letters to people I knew she knew in California hoping for more information about her.. No success and no response.

By the end of the year she wrote that she was in another movie "The Poppy is also a Flower" with Yul Bryner and Rita Hayworth. She also had a role in "Criterion Collection", "The Rose Tatoo" . "Woman of Straw" and many others by Fellini filmed in Italy.

My brother had another French girlfriend who he continued to see the following year but we never learned her name.

AUNT IN EUROPE

My Aunt Vera was in Europe and she reached Craig by telephone. They were to meet for coffee in a restaurant but he never showed. That night my aunt and her friend went to the theater to see a play. She saw a young man down front that looked like it might be my brother. He was with a exotic type woman that she thought to be Gilda. Her black hair was now blond. When the play was over she waited to see if her evaluation was correct. It was Craig and Gilda but they were too far from her to make contact. She said that he walked just like my father and grandfather. *(Much later that was verified when we visited. He walked like him, smoked a cigarette like him, talked like him, but also thought and acted like him. The family resemblance was uncanny.)*

MOTHER CORRESPONDS

Mother never lost hope and no matter what happened she professed with optimism that one-day things would be better. Now that we had an address, Mother continued to correspond to keep the gates open to her son. Gilda would write back with positive remarks about my brother's relationships, activities, schooling and associations. However as always, she purposely left out details like people's names or places. It was as though she had a sixth sense that I was watching and wanting that information. She would constantly remark about my father's stubbornness and that my brother was just like him. Evidently, this became a 'power tool' my brother effectively used against her to have some control over his life. Her letters were full of words to stimulate my parent's emotions.

CRAIG BEGINS RESEARCH FOR BOOK ON LBJ

It was June and Gilda came to Los Angeles, telephoned and advised me that Craig was busy researching information for Sam Houston Johnson for a book about his brother President Lyndon Johnson. She was obviously very excited about this and said that Sam was going to give honorable mention to Craig for his research. Later when the book "L.B.J." was published we purchased it. One of the first pages did give honorable mention to Craig Dahlberg for his research work. *(We now have Craig's autographed copy as well.)*

LETTER ARRIVES

Gilda wrote that another girlfriend had left Craig and he had turned off his telephone. She stated that he did not allow her to give out his address and stated that if I go to him, he might run from me. I thought that was a bit strange but never commented on it. Yet, she stated that he wanted to be reunited with his family. What a contrast and probably all a lie. By February he was in a hospital in France. April she wrote that Craig was in Mexico and writing a book and she might come to Los Angeles soon. When she arrived in Los Angeles she called my Uncle Milton and asked him to drive her to Palm Springs.

Instead there was a problem and she received a call to return to Mexico. She never revealed what that was all about. We were overjoyed Craig now was living a bit closer to us. She made numerous trips to Los Angeles, but never brought Craig with her. One time telephoned us to meet her for lunch. My husband Richard and I went, picked her up at a Beverly Hills Hotel and she suggested that we go to lunch at Denny's.

During lunch she made some statement that my grandparents minister approved her being Craig's guardian. I knew it was false. I said "No, that's not right." Her reply was very strong, "You were a child, you don't remember!" *(I did remember, I remembered more than she would ever give me credit!)* I could see that I agitated her. I sat in my passive mode for the rest of the lunch and just let her and my husband talk. When we had finished with lunch she pulled out her roll of dollar bills wrapped with a one hundred dollar bill, to pay for the lunch. Her eccentric way to make people believe she had a lot of money!

She invited us up to her room. Walking to her hotel from the parking space I notice the actor Van Johnson looking at us from across the street. (*A common thing for that area of town.)* We went to her little room and she asked me if I could shorten a skirt of hers. I said yes, and she got out some thread and I shortened the skirt.

In the meantime, she blew her nose and dropped the tissue on the floor. In fact I noticed there were a lot of tissues on the floor. Richard and I just looked at each other, and we knew what each other was thinking immediately! The phone rang and she talked to someone using words like "Darling". I finished shortening her skirt. Asking me shorten the skirt was to show me that *I was merely an underling and insignificant as far as she was concerned.* I understood because I had seen her do this to Mother and my Aunt Marion and others, before many times.

We wanted to establish a better relationship with her with the hope that one day we would be able to see my brother. We knew she was someone we needed to conquer with honesty and sincere kindness.

NEW ADOPTION PAPERS TO BE FILED IN FLORIDA

The only leverage that my parents felt they had was to "hold out" signing any adoption papers and giving her what she wanted most. They never did "give their son away" as they were accused of doing numerous times in legal papers and in the daily newspapers. They believed that someday he would come home and they could tell him the truth of what happened, if he wanted to know. Whatever he would have decided whether he was fourteen, eighteen, twenty-one or older, they would have honored. They realized that after years with this couple a bond had formed, possibly even a love and they were never out to destroy the son they loved, by trying to destroy what he sincerely felt in his heart for them.

Our parents were advised of the Legal Adoption Hearing for my brother in Palm Beach, Florida. . Our brother is now twenty-eight years old and able to sign his own adoption papers. This *presented a very hopeful opportunity* to be able to see my brother in person, so our mother and sister (now 18 and driving) went to Florida in hopes of making contact with him. Unfortunately, all the papers were pre-signed and Craig did not appear. Mother was very disappointed.

When Gilda saw Mother she became very nervous and excited. Mother did have an opportunity to tell the judge she was just there to see her son. Cheryl told me later that just looking into this woman's eyes was frightening. She had not seen her since she was a very small child. I couldn't have agreed more.

NOTARY FOR ADOPTION PAPERS

I wrote a letter to the notary of my brother's signature. I learned that he had never actually seen my brother and the papers were not signed while in his presence...This is contrary to our laws in the United States. The only person he had seen was the woman (Gilda) who had brought the signed papers into his office to notarize. I truly wondered and still wonder how legal those adoption papers actually were under such circumstances even though they were passed in Florida.

I would not however oppose them, because I believe he was entitled to whatever and it was her wish. She had become his so-called mother over all those years, regardless of our thoughts about it. Emotionally that is true.

GILDA AND CRAIG MOVE TO MEXICO

It was shortly after the adoption we learned that they had moved to Mexico. At least that was on this continent. Maybe now he would come home, maybe now she would let him go. All our hopes emerged only to be put on hold.

I wondered what card she was holding now. But it gave me some kind of hope that as adults we would be reunited. I hoped he would be a normal type person with an inquisitive spirit to venture home. I was only to be disillusioned in my dreams about the person I had hoped he would become. He may have been able to speak three languages, had a good education and met the most interesting people of the world, but he was also an intelligent person with a troubled soul and rightly so!

After this, I received another letter that my letter touched my brother's heart. Truth is she had won the battle of the adoption and she mentioned that she had wanted my mother to stay with her in Florida, when she was there. We knew that this arrangement would have been impossible. Mother never would expose my sister to the abuse we all had and was smart enough to never let her self get involved again.

Much like our family, our brother was quiet, timid, shy, gentle, fearful, and insecure in spite of all the wealth that surrounded his life. The hopes and dreams of our parents were that it would render his life so much more. He was not a courageous soul wanting to find answers. He never learned how to do for himself, make decisions and have a life for himself. He truly never fully developed his true potential and it was because of the forceful and controlling personality domineering in his life. His stature was slight, with blond hair and blue eyes. His lifestyle was chosen for him and was very worldly leading him into various types of addiction and sin.

YEARS SLIP BY….WITH SPASMODIC CONTACT

Mother, Aunt Marion and I were active volunteer members in the Children's Home Society, an Adoption Agency in Los Angeles. We loved the work they were doing on behalf of children. One year I was president and really matured in areas of leadership. Leading our local group was a real challenge for my quiet and withdrawn nature.

Later, I held a job as billing clerk for a local Insurance Agency and also a part time job giving jewelry parties. Richard was busy learning the building trade and advanced to "trouble shooter" for E.W. Hahn Construction in Hawthorne, Ca.

MOTHERHOOD

From the time I played with dolls I had looked forward to becoming a Mother. In my era, motherhood was the dream of every little girl. Watching and helping my own Mother and caring for my little sister Cheryl was the next thing to doing it. I enjoyed having a darling little child to take for walks in her buggy and have people be surprised that inside there was a real child.

My friend Cathy would take a neighbor child and I would take my sister Cheryl for rides in their buggies around the neighborhood and park. Sometimes we would walk to the corner drugstore and have a five-cent cherry coke. My friend always asked to push my pretty little sister because she was so beautiful.

When almost every woman marries she looks forward to motherhood. When it does not happen it can be a very distressing experience. It can affect some women acutely and they sink into depression. The disappointment was very devastating. That is what happened to me!

Pregnancy did not happen and the reality of the disappointment was almost too much. No one in my family was aware of how deeply the disappointment affected me. I realized my emotional condition was not right and I went to work hoping that being busy would help me get over it. Shortly after I needed medical advice and the doctor put me on tranquillizers to help me adjust. When I saw the doctor he suggested that I start going to church. I did not know how that would heal my hurting soul but ultimately it proved to be my answer.

I had some other medical problems that needed to be addressed and when they were cleared up the possibility was 9 to 1 chance of getting pregnant. "If" I ever would get pregnant, it would happen at the end of nine months." I had endometriosis. The doctor also recommended we check into adoption. Since I had worked as a volunteer with the Children's Home Society and was still a member of a local auxiliary. February we put in our application to adopt a child. I successfully hid my personal pains from everyone, even my husband and the social worker as we proceeded with our decision to adopt.

MY CENTER OF CONCERN NOW IS OUR FAMILY

Our own lives become very active and the center of concern. We had been married for four years and I was without child. We made plans for take a trip east to visit my husband's parents in North Carolina and to visit my grandparents in Minnesota during the Thanksgiving season. We decided that in February we would apply for adoption and shortly after that was completed, we would put an addition on our home.

By June our social worker told us that we were seriously being considered for a little girl and we were called in to have a little visit with her to see how we blended as a family. On June 24, 1966 we went to pick her up. What a blessed day that was for us.

We both were in heaven as we held this darling "bundle of joy". From the moment we held her in our arms, we loved her. I did not know that I was capable of loving a child more than anyone in the whole world.

My husband was now 30 years old and I was 28. We were very ready to devote our lives to raising and loving Linda and giving her the best of ourselves. We enjoyed every moment we had with her and we waited too long before inquiring about getting another child. It was too late, there was the pill and girls were beginning to keep their babies, so there were not as many children available.

(*Today, we thank God every day for the years we were able to have Linda with us. She is now a happy wife and mother of two wonderful blond blue eyed boys. Her eldest son, now thirteen and the youngest is eight. Her eldest son, now thirteen reminds me of my own brother. We are doubly blessed.)*

TELLING THE STORY ABOUT MY BROTHER TO A NEIGHBOR

When I finally did confide about my brother to a dear friend and neighbor she thought I was mentally ill and was conjuring up the story about my brother to get attention and it was all a lie. After she got to know me better she realized what I had shared with her was true and told me what she had thought previously. She is the one who took me to the self-help group when I told her. I knew I wasn't coping with the disappointment of not being able to have my own child as well as other issues in my life. I was working as a billing clerk for an insurance agency and asked to cut my hours at work, so I could attend the group. Attending and sharing, did help some to relieve my depression. I did not find lasting relief or healing for my problems.

Soon I learned that I had other issues I needed to deal with pertaining to my brother and other family related issues. During those months I became more aware of many things about myself. I learned better ways to handle my problems. All was not completely lost.

As I write this in relation to my brother, I must share the following: This is something I have never shared with anyone, but I feel it is so relevant to this story.

RE LIVED FEARS

The fear of having our daughter taken (kidnapped) from us was something that I lived with every day of her life. I was determined that no one was ever going to have a chance to do what was done to my parents. As a result, I could not help becoming an "over-protective" parent. She probably is a protective mother also. At least they are safe!

Some members in my family criticized me for being cautious, they never realized the underlying reason why my concern was so important to me. I am sure most mothers have concern for the welfare of her children but I was probably a bit more cautious. I have given this advice to our daughter. "You must do for your children what you can live with yourself." I told her this because that was my rule when making decisions where I was fearful for her safety. At times I am sure she felt I was too controlling because she used to ask me to just trust her. I tried to explain that I trusted her; I just didn't trust other people. How could I go into all the facets that caused me to be the way I was? I couldn't!!

Today our daughter is happily married. That did not eliminate experiencing those fears right away. I was confident and assured with all my heart that she was loved and would be protected by her husband and that gave me great comfort.

Those fears have subsided, but they continue to arise when I am with my grandsons and out shopping. Other times when the communication is poor between our daughter, I experience the agony of the old fears for short periods. When we are able to talk and I know things are going well for her and her family, I am at peace again. I am glad I recognize the source of these fears today.

(I have deep compassion for the "fears" that my parents endured and especially with what my mother lived with all those years. Because of the circumstances and the sufferings we experience, we become who we are. God can take the most unfortunate situations and bring good out of them to develop our character.)

My husband and I had looked forward to the roles of Mom and Dad since the early years of our marriage. Like many couples we were ill prepared to be "perfect parents" for this child, even though we loved her dearly and did the best we were able at the time. This darling bundle of joy was a full time job.

When our daughter was about three years old, I began to baby-sit a little boy up the street (Kenny). He was blond and cute just like my brother and he was a good playmate for our daughter even though he was a bit older. His parents invited us to go to church with them. It was the beginning of the school year and it was Sunday School Round-up time. The theme was western, so many of the people dressed in western clothing. We enjoyed the evening as they played guitars and sang a lot of old time gospel songs. We laughed and clapped hands and I could see the joy on the faces.

I had only attended Vacation Bible School in my childhood, and very little Sunday school. I did not know people who attended church could have so much fun. I began to visit the church now and then on Sundays. I felt so welcome and I began to hear things I had never heard before.

PART VII

Approximately..Six
Months Later...

DRASTIC TURN FOR THE BETTER...
ACQUAINTED WITH THE MOUNTAIN MOVER! !

Visiting this little church in Arcadia, Ca., hearing the sermons of Warren Anderson and being with people who really knew and loved God was something I had never known before and God touched my heart and I accepted Jesus Christ as my personal Savior and Lord and began my personal Journey to learn about God. I was challenged to be obedient to His Words and begin to take my trip on His roadmap for my life. I became aware I was changing as He miraculously healed and transformed my life by His mercy and grace. I began to understand about His love for me. Because of the things Mother had taught me about God, instinctively I knew He was my answer to everything! I needed to know Him and include Him in my life....

This may not seem relevant to the story about my brother, but it is because these events brought about a 'change in me' that ultimately caused me to experience God's "agape" love and that change is what has 'made the difference' in bringing about the personal contact with him, we wanted and desired for years!

GOD BEGAN TO CHANGE MY HEART
(partial-testimony)

This was my time! No one ever knows what course of events will take us to that place where we recognize our own person or where we recognize our own sin and shortcomings. God often allows pressures and stress to build up to get us to a place where we are willing to listen to Him and yield to His plan for our life. That is about where I was.

Once again the anxiety and reoccurring guilt and pain about the separation of my brother from our family was becoming acute. Now that I had a child of my own I began to realize a different kind of pain that my parents had experienced and I wanted to help relieve it any way I could. Craig's absence seemed very important to me and I wanted him to enjoy knowing our daughter.. Coupled with the complexities and daily problems of my marriage everything seemed impossible. I only shared my concerns with a few people in my attempt to find some solution to my dilemma. I went to Ala-non and Overeaters Anonymous and they introduced me again to the higher power (God) of my childhood.

Our darling little daughter needed security and stability in her life. I did not want who I was or what had happened to me and my own fears and anxieties to be any part of her life. I wanted to spare her every kind of unhappiness possible. I feared that my own sincere search for the truth and past involvement with cults somehow might touch her life, (I have long since denounced everyone of them). I became more aware of the phobic fears and how they had devastated and crippled me. I did not want this child I loved with my whole heart to be affected by any of this. I did my best to live, act and be normal regardless of what was happening in our lives. It was an impossible task but I tried!

There was something special about that little church and its people that kept drawing me to it. I would visit occasionally by myself, sitting in the back row. I was hearing a message I had never heard before on any Easter or Christmas when I went to church. I heard that I could have a brand new start in life. That all I had done in the past could and would be forgiven and forgotten by God. All I needed was to repent and ask Him.

The pastor spoke about becoming as a little child and about being "born again". I had never heard of such a thing before, but he explained what it meant in such a way that it was easy to understand. I felt a tug at my heart. Something inside of me just knew that is what I needed to happen to me. He quoted, what has come to be one of my very favorite verses, "Seek ye First the Kingdom of God and His righteousness and all these things shall be added unto you" from the book of Matthew. (6:33)

One Sunday as I sat in the back pew, hearing that I needed to accept Jesus as my personal Savior and that He would forgive my sin and I could start anew. We sang, "All He Wants Is You." My heart longed to know that God loved me and the only Scripture that had stuck with me all my life was John 3:16 “For God so loved the World He gave His only Begotten Son to die for me, and whosoever believed on Him He gave eternal life.” This Scripture I had memorized when a neighbor lady challenged the children in the neighborhood to learn it. It was like a “call” on my soul that day.

I did not know anything about altar-calls and this church did not have one, but every part of my being wanted to run down the aisle to that altar and give all of me to God. I was shy and fearful of making a spectacle of myself, so I did not do it.

The next morning came and I was all bound up with a strange type of fear that really scared me. I called the church office and told the secretary that I wanted to come in and talk to the pastor. I didn’t tell her I wanted to accept Christ…because that was like a foreign language to me. Using Jesus name freely was very unfamiliar to me.

The pastor had a meeting and I was asked to come in later in the afternoon. I agreed and when I hung up the feeling of rejection overwhelmed me and the disappointment was intense. I did a most unusual thing, which was really foreign to my basic nature. I picked up the phone and for some reason called back, telling his secretary that it was urgent and I had to see him before he left. He agreed and I went right to the church.

When I got to his office, he asked me a couple of questions and then he said. “Lets kneel and pray” Pray in front of him or anyone, how could I do it? But at that moment I knew that I wanted to go “God’s Way” more than anything else in the world. So we knelt and he said, “You pray first in your own words and then, I will pray.” I began, “Dear God, I want to go your way, I want to know you and walk with you. I have made a mess out of my life and I want it all to be different. Please send your “Light” into my life today, Amen.”

I did not know I was a sinner because, on the outside I was comparatively a so-called ‘good person’, but inside I was a mess. After that the Pastor prayed and he said, “I will say a prayer and you pray the prayer after me.” I prayed what is known as the “sinner’s prayer” and asked Jesus into my heart and life. I was a bit shocked to call myself a sinful person.

There were no flashing lights, no inner heat, no special feeling, nothing except I just ‘knew” that what I had done was totally right…I did not know until later that God’s Light is Jesus Christ. I learned more about that when a darling member of the church called and said she wanted to help me in my new walk with the Lord. A call she believed had come to her heart from God! I will be eternally grateful to God for speaking to her about me. She is still a blessing to me. My dearest friend in the entire world, my sister in Christ is Barbara Slater. She was my "lifeline" to learning about God and how much He loved me. She helped me draw on the power of God through His Word and to trust in and rely on Jesus for every circumstance of my entire life. She prayed with and for me.

Some days I had to call her several times because of the oppression I had lived under for years. The enemy of God was having his fun with my life and I was tormented for years. (I could expound on this much more because I lived it.) One time I had someone I love actually "laugh" at me when I said there was a devil. I assure you, he is real but he does not have the power to harm you unless you give it to him. Sin opens his door… God's power is much much greater!!!!!!

Barbara fed me Scripture that came alive in my heart and life. She explained what I didn't know. Some people wouldn't understand this statement, but I did not believe in the virgin birth of Jesus. My total belief in the virgin birth came miraculously into my spirit as I began to have a personal relationship with the person of Jesus Christ through prayer.

The faith God gave me began at the very moment I accepted Christ. In the early part of my journey with the Lord, He answered so many prayers quickly to increase my faith and trust in Him. My eyes and ears were opened to truth and life. The darkness that crippled my life began to disappear as more of God's Light filled its spaces.

Because I was in an honest pursuit like most people for enlightenment and truth and had made a decision about Jesus at about twelve years of age, God had his protective hand on my life. Because of the lack of spiritual guidance and direction, (ages 12 to 34) I became what we now know as "oppressed by Satan" (*Oppressed is just as devastating as Possession)* and possibly his old demons were terrorizing me. I was always accused of being super-sensitive and through that sensitivity he tried to torture me. The enemy hates those who accept Christ. He loves crippling or causing a Christian witness to become null and void. I had no witness at all, all of those years and finally I had reached out once again and took the Hand of God.

Previously my pursuit to find God was an "intellectual" one and when I meet people who are in all sorts of cults, I can spot the way they feel about me today right away. I used to feel the same way about people who found such an easy and simple faith. I have such compassion for them, they are "blinded just as I was by intellectualism". God made it so easy, so simple! People make it complicated. They honestly believe they are "intellectually superior" because of what they believe. My heart goes out to them, I know from the way I was, all I can do is remember them in prayer. My wonderful God loves them as He did me. As the song goes Just as I am. God's love through His Son is a Gift! We make it so hard and He offers it so freely ......all we need is to reach out and take Him into our hearts and lives.

The closer I walk with the Lord and abide in His Word, the more I am delivered of self and selfishness, the happier I become. It has been a glorious and wonderful adventure "getting to know God". Yes, there have been hard times of trials and suffering. But through all of that I have endured, for He has been with me all the time and I have learned so very much.

I tried to share my conversion with my family but they did not understand. The faith they had was different and not verbal. I was usually quiet person and all of a sudden I was different and using Jesus name freely and without reservation. . I was excited about what I had done and what had happened to me and I just openly shared it with anyone who would listen. Attending church and Bible studies became my lifestyle. I began to teach Sunday School, actively work in the church and then became our Missionary Women's President and actively served on the church school board and treasurer doing numerous other things through out the years. I had never known such happiness and freedom in all of my life!

A LOVING GOD
NOW
BEGINS TO MOVE THE MOUNTAIN
AND
PERFORM HIS WONDERS

PART VIII

New life in Christ births New Adventures of Answered Prayer!

AGAPE LOVE IS BIRTHED IN ME

It was July 24, 1968 that I made my decision. It was the following February just before Valentine's Day, the Pastor gave us a sermon about love. He said that he wanted us to experience love in the way God expects us to love others and he gave us a challenge of a lifetime. He gave us a challenge and asked, "Is there someone you really do not like or even hate?" Right away, I thought about this terrible woman who had taken my brother from my family. I did not like her. I possibly hated her. The Pastor challenged us to pray asking God to change our hearts to His kind of love for that person. I took the challenge!

By faith, I asked God to change the hate in my heart into His kind of love. The desire to try to manipulate her into getting what I wanted by carefully worded letters immediately left me. I prayed for God's "agape" love to fill my heart and I would have sincere forgiveness in my heart for her.

(Agape love is an in-spite-of anything and everything kind of love. No matter what you have done or what you will do, I will love you with the love of God, because that is the way He loves us.)

I really didn't know how all that would work or even how I would know that a change had taken place in my heart. I knew one thing and that was that I wanted to be in right standing with God. In order to do that, I had to also be in right standing with my fellow human beings. Forgiving Gilda I believed was a big order for God to give me but I laid all my dark hatred for her at the foot of Jesus Cross that day.

MIRACLE PHONE CALL

Four months later, the telephone rang. It was Gilda and I was so surprised she had kept our telephone number. I was even more amazed at what I felt inside, no fear, no hate but a sort of warm compassion I never had known before and I did not understand. I remember responding to her favorably and telling her I was really glad to hear from her. I asked her about herself and about Craig. Would it be possible for us to see her.

(*The Lord's love is always evident when we are willing to take the Challenges of His Word and applying the principles to our lives.)*

She told me it wasn't possible this visit but that she had a "picture of my brother" for me and she was going to mail it to me. I was so excited! ! We (Mom, Dad and I) did not know what my brother looked like as an adult and our last picture was of him when he was around twelve or thirteen years old. We did not have one picture of him all those years.

(*God always knows exactly what will bring us the greatest happiness.. and he is always more willing to give it than we ever realize.)*

I thanked her from the depths of my heart and told her how much it meant to me. She promised we would have more contact with each other.

After I hung up, I realized I was free from my fear of her. God had truly transformed those hateful feelings into His form of love. I had just experienced the "mighty loving power of God" in my life and my heart rejoiced and praised Him. I cannot say that I have forgotten all that happened to us or that the love that happened within me was the kind of love that holds no doubts or reservations, it does. It is a knowledge that regardless of everything, God loved her just as much as He loved me and it is my obligation out of love for Him to treat her with that kind of love as well.

I could hardly wait to report this expected gift from Gilda to my parents but I waited until I received the picture. I wanted to protect them from further disappointment and hurt in their lives. I don't think I was able to really share this story with them, but I knew a loving and wonderful God had changed me and blessed my life. In turn somehow what God had done in my life was also going to bless my parents. When the picture arrived I was so surprised to see the similarities of my father and my brother. I would have known him anywhere.

For Christmas that year I had an artist make a painting of my brother's face as a gift for my parents. It was just of his face and beautifully done. They really liked it and they hung it over their bed, probably symbolically of their unfulfilled desire to have him near to them.

Craig and Gilda

Letters from her came more frequently and although I no longer tried to manipulate her when I responded, her letters became more flowery and flattering and I was glad to get them. More consistent communication meant that I was making more progress in relating God's love to her by what I wrote in response to her letters. I hoped that my brother would also be given my letters to read.

They now lived at the same address and I took more care wording of my letters to him as well. I wrote about our daughter and the family, never really giving too much information. It seemed to work well and she continued to respond to my warmth and honesty. God is beginning to tear down the mountains of separation and my heart was full of appreciation to Him for His hand in my life.

GOD MOVES MORE MOUNTAINS!!!

SURPRISE TELEPHONE CALL

All of a sudden one day my brother called from Mexico and even gave us his telephone number. A picture of him received and now a phone call!! We chatted only a few minutes about family. He said, "I love you and miss you." and I said, "And I love you and miss you too." Short and sweet, that's how we like it! (*Astonishing how marvelous is the Lord's love for us, shown in so many ways! God's timing is always perfect. Yes, even if we have to wait a lifetime for His hand to move and answer our prayers. When His answer comes it is more precious than we ever imagined and even more of a blessing than we deserve.)*

At last the personal contact we all have longed for. This was the first indication that my brother actually 'wanted' our relationship established and to me it was a direct answer to prayer that I had prayed for a long time. Before this I was always the one reaching out with no response coming back. It was wonderful to hear him say, "I love you" too. Our talks were about politics, family or just chit chat, but that was more than we had exchanged in all those years.

LETTER TO BROTHER ABOUT NEW DAUGHTER

I wrote many letters to my brother about our new little daughter and all I was learning about becoming a mother. I sent him a picture of her. I told him everything I could about her. When she said, "Mommy, I love you" and how deeply that touched my heart to hear those words.

I wrote about how understanding a mother feels about her child, and a little about how Gilda must also feel about him, even though she was not his natural mother. Because we had adopted our daughter, I knew about loving a child deeply that was not born to me.

I wrote about how I loved doing all I could for our daughter and the sacrifice involved of ones time and energies. Remember, I am writing sincere letters and hope they will truly "touch her heart".

In 1968 she wrote back about how much my brother loves me and how he wanted to see me. I wrote back a letter telling her we would love to see her but financially we could not afford to do so. I swallowed my pride and asked her if she would purchase tickets for my husband and me and our daughter to go and visit them.

The truth is, I did not really believe her words or that she wanted me to have anything to do with my brother but I just took a chance she might have been sincere and had changed. I got absolutely no response to my only request in all my life for something material from her.

The next letter I wrote told her that my Uncle Milt was remarried to a lovely woman. In that letter I told her that I wanted to be honest with her. I told her I had never trusted her, a feeling I believed she had always had about us. I explained that all I ever have wanted—was to be in touch with my brother. I told her that in three years maybe we could go see them.

Communication continued with several notes and letters and some telephone calls without interruption or their moving further away from us. My brother liked to call in the middle of the night. One night he called and asked for our parents' telephone number and then called them. They were surprised and delighted and encouraged him to call as often as he wanted. Another mountain torn to the ground for them too! They didn't mind if he called in the middle of the night, in fact they encouraged him to do it again.

His call to them was like a "gift from heaven" and it truly was just that! God had smiled down on all of us that night.

RECONCILIATION AFTER 27 YEARS WITH CRAIG IN MEXICO

Autumn a letter with a weakly worded invitation to visit them in Mexico. It sounded like an invitation and so thanks to my husband and his quick wit, we grasped the opportunity to visit them. We were financially able to do this over a Thanksgiving weekend. My parents took care of our daughter and we took off to see Craig. We telephoned and let Gilda know our arrival time and flight into Mexico City.

Our arrival was like being in another world, a messed up world! The semi-small airport was full of people, hustling and bustling everywhere like ants. A young Mexican man (Angel) stood patiently outside with a sign with our names written on it. He spoke a little English and took us to a taxicab to go to the town of Cuernavaca.

The driver frightened me before we even got a block away from the airport. Someone was walking across the street and he hardly put on his brakes and missed them by an inch as I screamed! He thought it was pretty funny and got quite a kick out of making this American gal give a holler.

We found out that you take your life in your hands crossing streets in Mexico, so everyone rides. It was a long ride to the place where they lived. Up and down mountain roads and Angel explained things to us as we rode along.

Finally he told us that we were almost there. We stopped and at one glance at the entry of their home, I wondered if I might be imprisoned because of all the bars on the windows.

We walked up an alley type street and had to walk down another smaller alley to get to their front door. I wondered if my dad's suspicions were right and this was a trick. My first thought was our daughter and would we see her again? I realized that my imagination was on fire and talked to myself and said, "No… we are here because God wants us to be here and we are going to be reconciled back with my brother!"

Going inside all my fears dissipated. A servant answered the door and then announced our arrival to Gilda.. The home was decorated in interesting Mexican motif. Huge beautiful poinsettias graced the inside walls of the garden. A typical hacienda was beautiful with a huge pool and patio. The home displayed a lot of outdoor living as the rooms all came off the patio on one side. The living room area had a display of photos of Gilda with many famous people, much like homes I remembered as a child when visiting my brother. Each bedroom had its own bathroom.

Gilda welcomed us and instructed the servants to bring us some tea. Then she told us that Craig had disappeared a few days ago and they did not know where he was or when he would return. Old feelings of the past returned and I remembered so many other times disappointment surrounded anything that had to do with this woman for my parents and myself. The disappointment was tremendous after traveling so far. My heart was about to break in two, but my darling husband said, "Don't worry, honey, we will find him."

That night God had special plans and sent a real angel named Bill Meng over to the house and he said he would take us into Mexico City to all the places he knew Craig visited. He asked if I had a photograph and I did and gave it to him. *(Spiritually we were not at that place where we could just sit, wait and do nothing. Sometimes we just have not 'grown up' enough to be able to do that and merely trust the Lord with faith).*

The next morning Bill arrived in his beat-up Mustang that smelled of gasoline and off we went all the way back to Mexico City. The young teenage man whose name was "Angel" went with us and we walked through the worst parts of Mexico City. We had two angels with us, one on each side! We were told that some areas were where the drug addicts hung out. We went from store to store asking about Craig but no one had any information about my brother or else they were not revealing it to us.

A WHOLE DAY WASTED SEARCHING THE CITY.

To add to the problem, just as we rounded a corner a wheel of the car fell off and lug bolts went all over the street. Had that happened while we were on the mountain, who knows what would have happened. The car would not move and Bill and the young man ran between cars and found the lug bolts and put them back on. I stayed in the back seat and just prayed. Bill seemed so sincere in his attempt to help us.

We couldn't find my brother and so we went back to the house and had dinner. Bill and Angel went home. After dinner Gilda left us at the house and went out to a nightclub for the evening. Later she returned home with a party of people she had picked up. A young woman who looked a lot like and even sounded a bit like a popular black singer, a young white girl and man and one Mexican with a guitar. We were introduced and then.... they commenced to party smoking marijuana cigarettes..

I observed one of the young ladies had some raw marijuana and she invited me to go in the other room to watch her do something to it. It did not make any sense to me why Gilda would involve herself in this sort of thing. They began to smoke it and asked us if we would like to join them. Needless to say, we were not interested! What a putrid smell and it began to make me feel ill and I requested that my husband and I go to bed. It was truly one of the most terrifying nights of my married life because my husband said and did some bazaar things and I was sick all night long.

Finally my husband was sleeping soundly. I got deathly sick and I didn't know what to do. I had "Montezuma's revenge". Early in the morning I decided that Bill would know what to do. So I called Bill and he told me what to do. I sent the servant to the drugstore to purchase what he recommended. The maid gave me sour lemons to suck on and dry toast but the symptoms remained. I was scared and did not want my husband to leave me alone. I felt very weak.. I did not know how long this sickness would last and I wasn't sure why I was so sick and he wasn't.

REMEMBERING MY SPIRITUAL COUNSEL BACK HOME

I began to pray differently than I have ever prayed before doing what some might refer as rather fanatic. Before we left home I had time to share with a full gospel minister what kind of atmosphere we were going to be in and he gave me some Bible verses to claim and some spiritual advice regarding "Spiritual Warfare". I had put tags on the pages of Scriptures to read to give me courage. I literally felt the darkness all about Gilda's residence. I began to "plead the Blood of Jesus" and telling the enemy Satan to get lost. I confessed that the "Lord is in control of all that is going on" even if it all seemed out of control. I had Christian tracts with me and decided to put them all over Craig's room.

I began all this the minute I heard Satan tell me to just 'jump in the pool'. He knew I did not know how to swim.. I think when I heard that voice it really frightened me. I realized I was in his territory and became more convinced doing these extreme measures would be my only recourse to fight the dark forces around me.

Then, all-of-a-sudden I felt I sensed having better control and the peace of God filled me. His strength filled me and I felt stronger than I had ever felt in my life and I knew I was in His perfect will. It was an awesome feeling to know that. *The Presence of God will always fill us with His Peace!*

When you trust in and rely on God's power, fantastic things seem to happen as we put our complete trust in the Master-Creator! Understanding the darkness and evil that tried to destroy my parents lives, plus having the knowledge to combat it with God's Word and Power has increased my own faith time and time again.

LATE IN THE MORNING

Late in the morning Gilda awakened and her servants brought her breakfast in bed. For some reason I knocked on her door and she invited me into her room. When God's peace filled me, after prayer I felt spiritually strong so I bravely asked her if we could pray for my brother's return. She said, "yes " and so I prayed.

When I finished, she said rather indignant, " I am just as good at praying and God always answers my prayers." I recognized the "proud spirit" but did not comment or respond. I simply replied, "That was nice." and left her quarters. In fact, I hoped God might answer her prayers as well as mine!

At lunch, I thought it was very interesting when she asked me, "Why did you use Abraham and the Old Testament names when you prayed?" I said, "Well, I thought it would be more meaningful to you because you are Jewish." Right then, she told me, "I have never been Jewish in all my life." I was surprised because I remember my Uncle Milton had told the family she was Jewish and her family were Jewish as well.

(*I thought that was denial on her part but my passive nature never questions others and I had no basis other than overheard comments regarding her genealogy. I personally thought that heritage was super because Jesus was a Jew and Jews have a bloodline to the Messiah, gentiles are merely 'grafted in the family by adoption.. I am most grateful to our Jewish friends and to my Jewish Messiah.)*

GOOD NEWS…CRAIG IS FOUND

After lunch she said that she received a telephone call from someone she had looking for my brother and they had found him and he was in bad shape. She commented, "Our prayers are answered." We did not know what that all meant but we would see shortly. He arrived in about an hour and went directly to his bedroom to clean up with Gilda tagging right along behind him. A typical motherly gesture! A short time later, the doctor arrived and went into his room. Gilda came out telling us that my brother would be out to greet us in a while, the doctor had to examine him and he had to clean up.

When my brother walked in, our eyes met for just a second. I was a bit taken back with his appearance. He looked gaunt and years older than the photo that was sent to me.

(*I have seen Aids patients that had his look. But those days Aids was not known yet. He did not look well. He was very thin and his skin was gray looking.)*

I don't think that he really believed we were there! He may have thought he was having a dream or an hallucination. Twenty-seven years since we had seen one another. After all those years it was a bit overwhelming to him as well as to me.

I had an uncanny feeling that this was something he had wanted for a very long time and he was so full of emotion he was unable to contain or even express what he was feeling to me. Within a few minutes, he went back into his bedroom and later came out again. Possibly he was checking to see if all this was really true. He was not dreaming! He sat in the chair overlooking the pool smoking his cigarette. He seemed very quiet and deep in thought. His manner and actions were so like our dad's. He even looked like him but was smaller in stature, more like my mother's side of the family. We cordially exchanged small talk and greeted one another and my husband took some pictures of us. Gilda left us alone which I really appreciated. Then, he just got up and left the room again. I did not know exactly why he left me sitting there alone or even if he would return.

His disposition seemed so much like our dad but his actions appeared a bit rude. Possibly all this was getting to him emotionally more than I realized at the time. I know my heart was beating fast with the excitement of it all. I wanted to say so much but I am very much like our Dad and just couldn't stir up more emotion by verbalizing questions he might not want to answer.

If it were not for the support of my husband, it would have been too much for me too. I just wanted to be near him even if we didn't say a word!

It was not the kind of meeting I had dreamed and hoped for. Possibly we were too much alike. Even so, I was grateful. One I hoped and prayed my parents would also be able to have before too long. Maybe now he would come "home".

It was obvious the doctor had given my brother something, exactly what, I never did find out. Gilda talked about vitamins but I felt that was just her way of not revealing the truth to us. She had written that my brother had a serious problem with alcohol and a liver condition. It could have been that or something else that caused him to stay away from what he called home (and/or mother) so many times during his lifetime. Not once did she put him into a alcohol treatment center and she could have afforded to do it.

Later my brother came out again and we talked a little more and then, abruptly he left the house by himself. I wondered what on earth was he going to do? Was he going to leave permanently? I felt rejected and I asked my husband to follow him and see where he was going and what he would do. I didn't want to lose him now!

All he did was find an outside coffee shop, sit and have a cup of coffee, staring into space. Probably he was wondering why on earth I had entered into his life at this particular time. He did not seem to be ashamed of coming home in his condition. His knuckles were all scratched up as though he had fallen forward and his face was all full of cuts and bruises as though he had been in a fight. Or possibly someone had beaten him. He did not talk about it or give an explanation to us about what happened to him..

It was obvious to us that he was pretty messed up. I would have liked to take him home to California right then, I felt sure she would never let us do that. Even though the day before when we were out to lunch she offered to buy Red Crest Island in northern Minnesota for us if we would go there and take care of him. I wondered, Why an Island? I felt so proud when Richard told her that "he would not sell his soul for any one" and was very blunt with her and she amazingly took his direct answer! She had a lot of respect for Richard after that and often always acknowledged him as my husband and her friend.

It was interesting how from that moment she had her eyes on my husband and if she could she would have taken him as her son, lover, or whatever. I could sense by now, my presence was an irritation to her. Was it her conscience or what? I had always been some kind of irritation to her! I kept as quiet as possible and allowed her and my husband to talk about important things like money and politics or whatever she wanted to talk about with him.

The next afternoon, she took one of those nude sunbaths near the front entrance. My husband stayed in our bedroom until she was done and had returned to her quarters. She did have a cute little figure for a woman her age and was pushing near eighty. Gilda sincerely believed that she had some great power over all people. If she did not get her way, she would begin to yell and scream. Yet, she was so fearful that people might be going to steal from her. She had a knack for trusting all the wrong people who actually did steal from her, leaving my brother destitute. Possibly she was even murdered for it.

(*Strange thing, I feel a strange sense of "victory" because that money has never touched my life, I never was that needy. I never felt the greed to have to have it, all we ever wanted was my brother home with us. If he would have lived with us, it would have been nice for him to be able to contribute financially to keep his own independence.)*

Another friend of my brothers was also visiting in Mexico and Gilda introduced us to him. He had met Craig in France and was visiting with them. His name was Michael Van Der Goltz and he was on vacation. The day we were to leave she arranged for Michael to take us to lunch at a fancy hotel on the outskirts of town. It was beautiful setting in the hotel veranda. I never quite understood why she and my brother stayed home.

We thought that was a rather unusual way to treat house guests who were only there for a few days, especially after all that had happened we wanted to spend as much time with Craig as possible.

After lunch we went back to the house and found our bags packed and outside the door. To me that meant our visit was over and we were no longer welcome! My courageous husband said, "Let's go in and say goodbye!" So we walked right in behind Michael. They were having lunch on the patio. My brother looked puzzled and made some statement like, "Are you leaving already?" She looked a bit dismayed and I wondered what her explanation had been to him prior to our arrival. We went over bravely and thanked her and said goodbye to them both. About that time the taxi arrived and we were off to the airport in Mexico City to catch our plane.

We returned home and during the next year a cordial and friendly dialog of letters were exchanged. Her letters always seemed to hold a double meaning and often held slurs against my father in particular. I just ignored them but did not share them with my parents for fear of causing them more pain and hurt. If I did share anything Daddy would always say to me, "Well, just consider the source" in evaluating things. When the letters were nice, I would bring them to my parents home and let them read them. Others remained in my safe keeping. My parents had gone through enough, I wanted to spare them any more anguish.

Good Communication Continues

MIDNIGHT CALLS

Craig continued to call in the middle of the night. One time he asked, "What is the trinity?" and I explained. "The trinity is God the Father, Jesus the Son, and the Holy Spirit." I went on to tell him "God is three persons in one. All are a part of one God. Just like he was a son, a brother and maybe someday a father." Normally I might not ask this question but it seemed very appropriate to do so. I asked him if he had ever accepted Jesus Christ as his personal Savior and he said, "Yes, I have." I never questioned him any further. If people want to tell you more they usually will just do it then.

Another time, he seemed paranoid and told me to call the FBI. He said that someone was bugging his telephone. I don't know what that was all about but I did what he asked me to do, hoping they would check it out.

Other times the calls were just affectionate saying he loved us, often times they were very short calls, but having him telephone us brought so much happiness and contentment into all our lives. It was so wonderful to hear his voice. These years were so much better than previous years because I knew God was in control and was working things out. I rested in Jesus Christ. He became my place of refuges and strength and my hope for tomorrow. I knew in the end we would win the battle. I did not know how or when, but I knew deep within.. it was so. I began to pray for God to move the mountains of years of pain and suffering for my parents, my brother and me. I had claimed the promises I knew. I had asked the Lord to always be with my brother. I prayed for the Lord's Angels to encamp around him and keep him safe. I prayed for God's perfect will to prevail in all our lives. I had every reason (faith) to believe that in God's timetable. He would answer in a way that was best.

1979 GILDA DIES AND LEAVES BROTHER DESTITUTE.

The following information we did not learn until much later, but I am inserting it here to keep events chronologically in order.

The story goes like this: My brother was with a servant in his quarters. The reason is unknown. It was the middle of the night and Gilda rang for the servant to come to her aid. The cord to the buzzer was wrapped around her arm and somehow she had pulled the lamp down on her bed. The bed caught fire and she screamed and yelled. Finally the servant heard her and saw the room ablaze and ran to her aid. He pulled her and the mattress into the swimming pool and called the fire department. She was burned very badly and the doctors at the hospital could not save her. She died within hours.

My brother was arrested and put in jail. After a few days he was released.

Regardless of what I have commented about Gilda, without a doubt she truly loved my brother as a son. Her love may have been misplaced, distorted or obsessive and she did things wrong and hurt our family deeply. What a horrible and painful way for anyone to die. I am sure it was never her intent to leave my brother without any means of shelter or finances to feed and clothe himself. If anyone ever turned over in their grave, I am sure that she must have after the series of events that followed her death. She had provided for him all of his life and she willingly would have continued that for years more. The one thing I never understood was why she never taught him how to handle finances when he was to be her legal heir? That puzzles me to this day. Possibly she never wanted him to become "independent" of her even after death. Teaching a child to provide for himself and learn the skills of survival is what a good parent does.

I question if she just did not do it because she didn't think he had the ability or was it because he had an " attitude problem" about the power that money had had over his destiny and the separation with our family because of it. From information we have learned we believe the later is true. She had tremendous respect for the life her riches had brought her from what she shared with Richard and me when we visited in Mexico a few years prior. There are so many questions I will never know the answer to. So many wasted years!)

We were told that her attorney came down after she died and gave my brother $500.00 and that was all. When that ran out he had no food, no money and assumedly did not know how to obtain any because the banks had locked the accounts and he could not withdraw funds. When my husband Richard was checking the bank accounts he found $200,000.00 in one account. We never heard from anyone regarding these accounts.

Before the attorney left Mexico after Gilda had died, he had the servant drive all her worldly personal possessions to Florida via Brownsville, Texas. We were told that Norman and Craig had a 'garage sale' and sold items around the house for near nothing in order to get money for his food and shelter.

Friends my brother had met on the street came to his aid. Meg Donahey let him have a room and fed him. Norman Thomas fed him and put the food bill on his charge accounts. Craig was supposedly well liked around the town. They sincerely expected future compensation believing he was heir to millions of dollars. In the end, possibly some of them did get it from the Mexican courts!

Three months before she died, Gilda had consulted with an attorney in California but we never learned exactly what it involved. We did learn the following. An attorney in Mexico had her sign over stocks and bonds and a safety deposit box to him and he had the key. It seems that he obtained her power of attorney and had stocks and bonds changed into his name. When she found out she was outraged. How he was able to influence her and obtained this we are not sure. She was getting old and possibly her mind was not as sharp as it used to be. We assume he became her heir by default. When she learned that bonds that were hers, were in his name she became very upset. She hired a woman attorney from Los Angeles.

Shortly after she died in an accident! Who was to blame? Was it an accident or was she murdered? We understand the case remains unsolved.

PART IX

Craig is Hospitalized –
Destitute, Paralyzed and with Terminal Cancer in Mexico. ..
We go to his aid

CRAIG IS PARALYZED AND IN THE HOSPITAL

It was July 1980, and our telephone rang. A voice of a woman on the other end told us that she was a friend of Gilda's and Craig's and her name was Meg Donahey. She said, "I found your telephone number among some papers. I think you would like to know that your brother is in the hospital here in Cuernavaca. He is in bad shape and paralyzed from the waist down." I asked for the name and address of the hospital and the telephone number and she gave them to me. I said, "We will be in touch with him right away and see what we can do. I really appreciate your calling me and thanked her—saying—I hope we will be able to meet someday.". (If it were not for this Ms. Donahey's kindness this story might have had a very tragic ending.) We learned later that she actually had taken him in her home and supported him after Gilda's death and he was destitute, without shelter, food or finances.

Immediately after her call, we called my brother Craig in Mexico to inquire how he was doing. We told him about the phone call from his friend Meg and what she had told us about his condition. He sounded pretty good and very much like our dad. When asked how things were, he said, "Oh, they are going to be just fine." I could not imagine how he could say such a thing in the condition he was in, paralyzed from the waist down. My husband informed Craig, "We will be down to see you in a day or so". We don't think that he really believed us. We ended by both saying, "I love you" and Richard proceeded in making plans to leave as soon as possible.

My uncle Bob had just died very unexpectedly in Mesa, Arizona and my parents had gone there to be with Dad's sister Vera. We telephoned my folks there and told Dad about my brother. Dad seemed to think that if Craig said that he would be all right, he would be! Past experience now caused him to be cautious and especially protective of the family he had left. They would be home from Arizona in about a week.

For the first time in all my life, I heard myself disagreeing with my dad. (I never openly differed from my dad on anything.) I replied, "You know how we are Dad, we never really admit that we are in need and suffering. I do not believe Craig is any different and he definitely needs us now!" That was the gift of God's wonderful discernment in operation and I believed our family characteristics were alike and in the end, I was right!

I was so pleased when my husband told Dad we were going to Mexico to see what we could do to help my brother. Even though Dad never told us, I do believe he was glad we felt that way too and were able to do something for Craig. The three of us (Richard, our daughter Linda and I) left that Monday evening and arrived Tuesday morning (7a.m.) in Mexico City. We had no sleep and it seemed like a long arduous flight.

Before we left we decided that we should call an attorney in Florida. He had assisted Gilda years before and was Gilda's nephew. We hoped he might be able to help us with Craig. He agreed and told us he would meet us there giving us the name of the hotel where he would be staying. At this time we knew nothing about his previous trip or what had occurred after Gilda's death.

When we arrived, we could not find a cab anywhere and inquired how we could get to Cuernavaca. We learned there was a bus station nearby and we could take a "Cattle Bus" from Mexico City to Cuernavaca . It was full of people and a very old bus. It was a long two-hour ride. When we arrived in Cuernavaca we caught a cab and went to the hotel the attorney recommended and we also registered to stay there. It was a lovely place with tables around a grassy area with a fountain and the rooms surrounding the outside walls.

Cuernavaca has all the qualities of a small town. It seems that news travels very fast among its residents. Later everyone who had befriended my brother began to arrive. Each one related stories about my brother and what had happened to both him and Gilda. Each one desired to find favor in our eyes and we discerned their neediness for recognition, appreciation and some remuneration.

First we visited with the attorney and the lady Meg who talked to us over morning coffee. Then we left for the hospital to visit my

Craig. My husband did most of the talking and we determined we would see what the prognosis revealed after we saw the doctor.

Craig was so glad to see us. He seemed delightfully surprised and said, "Oh, I am so glad you are here." Richard replied, "Craig, I told you we would be here, Marlys and I always do what we say we will do, that is how we live our lives." At that Craig smiled and said, "Thank you so much for coming." He told us that he was aware that his body was in serious trouble.

We were left alone in the room with my brother and we asked, "Would you like to go home with us?" and he equivocally said , "Yes!" My heart must have jumped for joy at that moment! He actually wanted to go home with us, just what I had prayed for a million times in the years that had passed.. I could hardly believe what was happening, I questioned in my heart "if" it was really going to finally happen? A few years before the Scripture promise spoke to my heart. It states, "Delight thyself in the Lord and He shall give you the desires of your heart." The one desire of my heart was unfolding and I was actually a part of it after all these years. We were walking in the realm of something miraculous. I could sense God's presence and divine will for our lives and it was awesome!

Within minutes we talked to the doctor in charge and he told us that Craig needed surgery very soon. He explained his problem could possibly be cancer. He said that his convalescing time would be lengthy and he could not stay in Mexico. I told him that I wanted it done in the United States, not Mexico. It appeared everyone was going to be cooperative, and the doctor said that he would help with ambulance arrangements to travel to airport.

When Richard and Bill tried to get tickets from local travel agencies they ran into one roadblock after another. It was as though the enemy was once again trying to keep our family apart..

WE RETURNED TO THE HOTEL

After visiting my brother, we went to the hotel and had some lunch on the lovely veranda overlooking a water fountain in grassy area. The attorney, Meg, Richard and I discussed how we would get my brother to the United States. The attorney said, "Craig should go the Mt Siani Hospital in Beverly Hills. It is a well-known hospital and he called around unable to make any headway. Personally I was glad because I wanted him closer to our home so I could spend time with him and not have to travel fifty miles to visit. It would be like leaving him alone once again.

Then, as though out of thin air!. our old "angel" Bill turned up. We had met Bill on our first visit to Cuernavaca a few years before and he was a Godsend in helping us then. What a wonderful sight he was. This could not be coincidence, but the sovereign hand of God. Richard and I had casually talked about this being a divine appointment for us and in the course of events that follow we were assured it certainly was all of that and more.

The Lord had caused Bill to take this trip just at the right time and here he was once again to play a very important role in this scenario. Bill spoke Spanish fluently and was married to a lovely Mexican lady whose family lived nearby. Bill was a mult-talented musician and entertainer but seemed to be a 'jack of all trades' and had a heart of gold when it came to helping people. He told us his brother was a minister in San Jose, California.

Bill was a good person and by all indications he was a believer but lived a rather unusual vagabond type lifestyle living in Brownsville, Texas and traveling to various places in Mexico.. A lifestyle he enjoyed and made him happy.

ROADBLOCKS

Mountains or roadblocks we weren't sure. Trying to get tickets from the travel agencies in Cuernavaca seemed impossible. The travel agencies claimed it took a couple of days. Every travel agency Richard and Bill went to in Cuernavaca had one excuse or another for not being able to secure airline tickets. My husband immediately took charge and had an idea and called our doctor and the travel agency at home. They were happy to assist us and they made all the reservations and arrangements. The doctor approved and arranged for an ambulance to meet us at the airport in Los Angeles and take us to a local hospital.

Now, where is Craig's passport and papers? His passport expired in February 1980. My husband handled all of that and he was determined that Craig would be going home with us, papers or no papers! Bill supported the idea and agreed that he would translate whatever Richard wanted to say to the airport authorities in order to get us on our way.

My darling husband knew how much this meant to me and to my parents and absolutely nothing was going to stand in his way of doing it for us. Between our doctor and the travel agent everything was arranged and when it was time to go they called us at the hotel. The next challenge is in sight! We must all get to the airport in Mexico City. Somehow we had to get on that plane without a passport or a visa for Craig and pick up the necessary sixteen seats for his gurney, attorney and the three of us. We needed a total of twenty seats for five. Not an easy task, but with God "all things are possible" to those who love Him.

We had just finished breakfast when the artist by the name of Norman Thomas came in to meet us. He told us that he did not want my brother to leave Mexico. He loved him. (At that moment, I really didn't think about what he meant by that or the possibility his being gay.) I told him very persuasively, "This was both my brother's wish to go home with us and mine as well. He was leaving with us and we loved him too!"

Norman Thomas wanted to impress us and said that he had some painting hanging in a famous place. He said that he had painted the insignia for the Coast Guard during World s II and had that to his credit. His ex-wife was either the daughter of or was married to the Governor of Cuernavaca.

This man then said to me, "I will put a curse on you if you take Craig away from here." Years ago, this might have frightened me, but I laughed and replied, "In no way do you have the power to do such a thing to me or my family. I am a child of God and Jesus Christ is my Savior and I have more power than you do every day of the week." He was a bit taken back by my words. I think he must have realized he could not frighten me. From the stories he had heard he might have believed me to be as naive and fearful as my parents had been in their youth. From that moment on, I decided that I did not wish to be around Mr. Thomas and told my husband. Anyone that would threaten me is "checked off my list" of people I do not choose to associate.

He left the scene and we thought we were allowed to proceed with the plans. He showed up at the hotel just before we were to leave for his "payoff" from the attorney of $500.00 Norman said my brother owed him. He paid him in full!

LETS ALL GO 'HOME'

The next day we all met at the hospital where Craig was anxiously waiting. I don't think he really believed us when we told him we would take him home to California. So many times in the years past he was cheated of really going home.

Finally the ambulance arrived. It was like an old Helms bakery truck that used to go up and down residential streets of California in the 50's. It was made into a make shift ambulance with just a folding chair. The old gurney was brought in, Craig was put on it and it was decided that my husband would accompany him on the ride to the airport in Mexico City. They tied the gurney to something to keep it from slipping and sliding all over inside the ambulance. Richard and Craig had to hold on during the long ride to Mexico City. The attorney, Linda and I rode in the car with Bill. The ambulance started out first and we lost it somewhere along the route. Horrible thoughts rushed through my mind. I immediately covered them with prayer as we rode in Bills car to the airport in Mexico City.

When we arrived the ambulance with Richard and Craig was miraculously waiting for us at the airport. My brother stayed in the ambulance and waited his transport to the plane. The wait was longer and longer and he must have wondered if Gilda's ghost was once again going to cheat him from returning home forever. Our daughter and I waited in the small waiting section of the airlines. The attorney was here and there, Bill and Richard went to the appropriate places to get clearance for Craig to leave on the airline. My husband told (with Bill translating) the airport Police and Security that Craig was going home with us—as well as the airline authorities that an ambulance and doctor's and hospital were standing ready to receive us at the Los Angeles Airport. It it was 5:30 a.m. and took over six hours of persistent negotiation as we held up a planeload of anxious passengers..

I tried to keep our daughter entertained by telling stories, singing songs, drawing and taking short walks. It was not easy waiting for such a long time with a young child.

We were the only people waiting to get on the plane that was waiting for us to board. There wasn't even a place nearby to pick up a snack. I really appreciated having a little daughter with me, who loved Jesus, it helped me keep my mind focused and it helped to storm away my fears. She was exceptionally good for a little one.

MOUNTAIN MOVING PRAYERS!

While we waited and waited I kept claiming the promise, "God can move away a mountain if we have just the faith of a tiny mustard seed!, Nothing is impossible for God, and His Presence is with us when two or three agree on anything" I reminded God that those Scriptures really meant something to me and I believed He had control of all that was happening, even if it seemed out of control. During this time I also did what some Christians might consider a bit fanatic. I called on the God of possibilities for help. I kept praying binding the strong man (evil one) and pleading the Precious Blood of Jesus to cover all of us. I told "old slufoot" that he no longer had the right to my brother's life. I continued to believe God would give us the victory over all these (mountains) circumstances.

(My personal prayer reached into the heart of God to move in with His power! There is always unlimited power in the Blood of Jesus Christ when we claim it.. His blood has Healing Power, Delivering power, Protective Power and Sealing Power.

I had never before really 'felt' or fully understood what it meant to be in God's Perfect Will so profoundly. It was like receiving His call and being on a mission! I sensed the deep loving concern of my husband. Later he told me that he felt strongly it was a call on his life to bring it about as well.

The officials argued for hours and hours, saying, " No". One thing or another delayed our leaving. Craig's passport had expired, it was no good! Bill was translating for Richard in the passport office. Then, immigration was not going to let us through. Bill told them that my brother's life was at stake and only God and Bill really know what else he said. He argued fearlessly for us. Once my husband came up to check on us and told me that he was not sure if the elements back in that little town were trying to keep us from leaving. He encouraged me to continue praying hard for our departure.

Then, my determined husband told Bill to tell them, "Do you want this man's life blood on their souls when you die? Craig had to get to the United States for needed surgery in order to live and time was urgent according to the doctor in the Mexican town." My brother did not have a passport, visa or any travel papers and that was a part of their very valid argument. Then, all of a sudden they agreed to let us go aboard the plane.

(*We believed that God had intervened and miraculously changed their minds.)*

Finally we were led to the place where we were to board the plane. Then, they changed planes and we waited and waited because a stretcher was to be on the plane for us and it was not there.

After two more hours Bill negotiated for us to rent the gurney from the Mexican Ambulance drivers and we would return it with the next plane back. Sixteen seats had to be removed on the plane in order to take the gurney with my brother on it.. Finally, exhausted we were allowed to board the plane. We thanked Bill and he left. Our Mountain of Separation is removed at last! A sense of "victory" over all those years. Our parents only saw defeat in the things they tried to reconcile our family. An Awesome and Wonderful God did it all using vessels He choose for this time and this place. To Him go All Honor, Thanks and Glory!

Yes, It was a Miracle! !"

WE ARE ON OUR WAY!

As we boarded the plane I glanced over at Craig and saw him looking at us. That look said "Thank you from the depth of his heart." I could read in his eyes just how he deeply appreciated his deliverance from the life that had held him prisoner for all too long. A life that was empty of the love he needed and held little or no real meaningful purpose. A life lacking that family love every human being thrives on. He was glad to be going home!

Our biggest mountain is nearly removed!!

(*At the moment the plane took off we did not realize all the power of God had accomplished on our behalf. We were told that it was impossible and you cannot get remains of a dead person on a plane in Mexico without a passport or visa!!! The attorney told us that he could not even take the Gilda's cremated remains back to Florida with- out a passport or a visa. And here we were "in flight" on our way home to California.)*

We sat quietly for a while and then a surge of happiness filled my heart. What a wonderful Lord Who loves us all. In flight a new Joy filled our hearts. Mission almost accomplished!!

Half way to Los Angeles, Craig looked over at me again and said, " I can hardly believe this is happening, I am so happy to be going home" I knew what he meant and I wondered how many years that longing had been in his heart as it had been in mine. I don't think we ever told him the complete story of just how the Lord worked through Richard and Bill to cause it to actually happen because everyone was totally exhausted.

Most everyone underestimates what God can do through a willing vessel. There has never been anyone like my husband in my family and as year after year passes (now 43) I am very aware of just why the Lord sent him into my life. The Power and Goodness of God is my continued Blessing through him who loves me the way Christ loves the church. There isn't any greater love than that!

Reconciliation with all the family

BROTHER ARRIVES AT HOSPITAL…."HOME AT LAST"

Our doctor in Temple City saw Craig and called in other doctors. The doctor who was to do the spinal surgery noticed a lump on his neck and said, "Before we go in and do this, I want a biopsy of that lump, will you give your permission?" I agreed only to learn the next day that my brother's body was filled with cancer and that he had only days to live.

The news was devastating to me and the doctors could not give us a length of time we could plan on having my brother with us. The doctor did say, "If there were any complications like kidney failure or pneumonia the time would be shortened." We knew it was not too long but his death was eminent. We would work toward making him as comfortable as possible. They gave him radiation to eliminate some of the pain. After a couple weeks they talked about transferring him to a rest home. This meant that he never would actually be in either our home or our parent's home again. Home to California and with his family was all we could hope for in the days ahead.

Just three years before our dad was diagnosed with throat cancer and given three months to live. He had outlived their diagnosis and three years had passed. Now my Craig was given almost the same diagnosis with even less time than three months and he was paralyzed as well. Both Dad and my brother were smokers and both their deaths were attributed to that fact.

I questioned why God had brought us this far and now, we would have to part once again, forever. I was not really willing to accept it and I prayed and prayed. I wanted another miracle, one that would turn death into life. However, that was not the plan of God.

What if the doctor in Mexico would have insisted on keeping him there? What if I had not challenged the older man's threat of putting a curse on me and become frightened? What if my husband had not taken control? What if (our angel) Bill had not arrived? What if the attorney had not come and was able to pay-off the older man and the lady who made financial claims about their financial care of my brother prior to this happening? What if the airport people had not allowed him to come home? More "what ifs " continued filling my mind at a later time. Too many ifs . But by God's Sovereign Power and Love, He changed all the "ifs" in to possibilities and miracles. *Mountains called impossibilities, removed forever by His love and power!*

At the hospital the attorney said, "Marlys, you must talk to Craig about making out a will." I asked, "Why should I do that?" He said, "After all Gilda has assets everywhere and you need to protect Craig's inheritance." I replied, "I really feel uncomfortable talking to him about such things but if you insist that it is necessary I will do it." He told me what to ask him and when I was finished, he talked to him about it and had it made out and signed before he left town. The only land my brother had in his name in Palm Desert, California, Craig deeded over to the attorney to take care of the monies returned to the people in Mexico and to pay for his legal services. Craig left the rest of his estate to Mother and Dad. The attorneys, someone in Mexico or the government took it all. *(But as the affairs of Gilda's Estate were settled, nothing was ever given to Craig or his heirs. It is still a mystery to us and we assume that everything just reverted to her family in Florida, lawyers, Norman Thomas or to the Mexican government. The Palm Desert property was the only thing in Craig's name. When we got to California, attorney had Craig sign it over to someone in his family as payment for monies given him after Gilda's death as well as advising Craig to make out a new will giving his estate to Mother and his natural family. Richard was named as the Administrator of the Will. A useless will. We never saw a dime!*

Craig gave Richard Power of Attorney and when he went to Mexico to help clear up Craig's affairs he learned that Norman Thomas visited Craig in the hospital in California in the middle of the night and had him sign a will leaving his estate to him. Living in Mexico and speaking the language gave him an edge to claiming what-ever was there.)

Our parents came home in about a week from Arizona surprised and delighted that we had brought Craig back home with us. . My dad's sister Vera came with them. I was so pre-occupied with my brother I probably was not as thoughtful of what she had just experienced in the loss of her husband. I have often thought about that through the years but I know she understood. Our family is like that!

The first two weeks my brother requested that I call our parents and tell them not to come and visit because he would get too emotional. I honored his request the most tactful way possible and my parents complied. I think they understood. After being separated all those thirty-seven (37) years it was an emotional time for all of us. I wanted my parents to be granted full visiting privileges and now, my brother was making this request. I was not totally sure of his motives. I was more concerned about hurting our parents whom I loved dearly. I could not do anything about it. We just had to wait for a right time. The next time I talked with my sister and just said I couldn't reach them. That was the last time he told me to call them and say that.

Finally there was an opportunity to share with him that they were not going to cause a scene, ask him any embarrassing questions, make any accusations or even say anything against the couple that took him from us. I told him that if he wanted to ask anything, he would have to initiate what was to be discussed. Just like my Dad he made no comment at all, absolutely no response and in our way that sort of means. "I understand and appreciate that." I shared with him that they loved him very much and that it gave them great joy to just be in his presence even if he did not want to talk to them. They have waited for this time for many many years.

Oh yes, so many years, so many questions about his life left unanswered and not shared, but no one would disturb what had been unless he wanted it that way. This took place about two weeks after almost solid silence and a lot of television. It was as though he was evaluating and testing each one of us to see if we were made out of the same stuff as he was. (*Throughout the next month and a half Craig was in the hospital, he lovingly would squeeze my hand and we both instinctively knew exactly what it meant. "I love you always." For him it was "I love you and appreciated all you and Richard have done for me")*.

Our kid sister Cheryl who did not remember him, visited with her family. At first it was like testing the waters for all of them, then came the warmth that was very obvious to me as acceptance and love dominated everyone's visits. .

The third week came and our pastor, Drell Butler of Arcadia Community Church had visited him almost every day up to that time with just friendly get acquainted conversation. But today was different. Today he closed the door and he and my brother talked alone. Craig assured him that he had made his peace with God and that Jesus was His personal Savior and he understood even though he had hardly ever attended church in all his life.

From that day on, my brother seemed to have a deep peace and serenity and was more willing to share his love, which gave each of us 'something to remember'. I remember one day Mom and Dad came around the corner. My brother's face lit up and he said, "Here's the folks"! He was delighted to see them. He began to be filled with a new kind of contentment and happiness I don't believe he had ever experienced in his whole life. The folks would stay for four to six hours every day just to be near him, loving him and enjoying whatever tiny bit of himself he was able to share that day.

I could hear my brother and Dad having some father-son talks which I know blessed both of them. Mom and he would have different kind of talks and they were so special to her. He would reach for her for a hug and kiss and the affection gave them both a sense of happiness and joy. Something within myself gave me satisfaction as I sat around the corner and observed this reunion.

Dad had a chance to talk to him about his own cancer and what they did for him. I am sure giving Craig as much hope as was possible, even though they knew both ultimately it was terminal. Dad was given only three months and was still alive eight years later. All the doctors could do was give my brother radiation to relieve the pain and a promise of only a few weeks of life. He never had any pain but he did seem a bit anxious at times because he could not seem to watch a television program through. He would continuously switch the channels back and forth. He would ask for juice occasionally and we were allowed to go to the refrigerator and serve him.

My brother was a quiet type person and his temperament was like our family. We understood each other with very few words. We could all be in a room, find no need to even talk, just being together was satisfying. Some families would find that hard to understand but we were always a quiet peaceful people and when tragedy hit us, it never changed our temperament, if anything we become more quiet avoiding the emotional impact it had on each of us, always considerate of one another.

One day while visiting my brother he told me a story about himself that I will never forget. It was one of the times he just took off and left the comfort of the wealthy lady's home. Away from Gilda he said, "I was walking along some road in Mexico. I was hot and tired so I decided to lay down and rest a few minutes. I woke to a Mexican man with a large sombrero on his head standing over me. He asks me if I was all right? Then he invited me up the hill to what I thought was his home. I stayed there a couple weeks and enjoyed myself." Craig said to me, "You know what?" I said, "What?" and he replied "That the man had A.A. meetings every night in his house." I replied, "Wasn't that wonderful"? My brother said, "I was very happy there and did not want to leave, but I had to go." I wondered if this Mexican man could have been an angel, a real angel from the Lord that I had remembered praying would help my brother. I could not tell him about my prayers because he would not have understood. But God knew.

Most of the time I spent with my brother, my spirit was grieved inwardly because I really wanted to share my faith, but somehow there were no open places or green lights. No real freedom to do it. No indications from the Holy Spirit that I should speak. I was to just live my faith and lovingly care for him. I had a sense that he knew already. Those hand squeezes and the look in his eyes made me feel like his big sister again.

My special times with my brother were in the evenings from 6 to 10 p.m. I would just sit and watch television with him. Sometimes during the evening he would reach over for my hand and hold it for up to a half hour. He would squeeze it and I would squeeze back. That was our unspoken conversation of love and joy to just be together again. I wanted to ask him so many questions about his life but I could sense his great happiness was in just living for the moment. I decided to just leave the past buried forever in our memories.

The doctors told us that the radiation would relieve any pain and stress on his body. It would not cure, but only make the life he had left a bit easier for him. My brother had as much radiation as was possible.

My husband made a couple of trips to Mexico to try to straighten up his affairs and get his things and papers. He was led from one dead end to another. The police had confiscated personal items, stocks, and gold mines. The money in the banks was frozen. The post office box was pilfered and we could not get anything more from it even though my husband had all the proper papers to do it.

While he was gone the hospital insisted that my brother be moved to a convalescent hospital. When he got settled the room was hot and had very little ventilation. I was not happy with the services he received. He was supposed to be turned over every two hours to avoid pneumonia and he appeared to be drugged more than he had been in the hospital. They were always late in coming to care for him and said they were understaffed. I questioned what they were giving to him and could not get a straight answer. Within a few days my brother became incoherent and difficult but was still able to relate exactly what was wrong. Two times he pulled out the catheter, another time he flung his arm and knocked the food on the floor.

Craig began to tell me about Bror, Gilda's husband who had passed away and he said, "Bror came to see me last night." Fortunately I had heard of this phenomenon when people are about to pass over so I agreed, and I told him, "But not in the same way you see me, right?" He agreed and seemed pleased that I believed him and understood what he was telling me. I said, "You remember, he had already died." He said, "Yes I know!" I asked him if the man was good to him and he said, "Yes" and then I asked him if he missed him and he said, "Yes' again. I asked how he felt when the man died and he said, "It was awful, Gilda had yelled and screamed all over the hospital. Craig said it bothered him and he just couldn't forget it." I told him, "You know Craig, Jesus is in you and Jesus is in me and when Jesus is in us, there is no need for any of that because His love enfolds us." He said, "Yes Sis, I believe you, I know you are right." At that point I caressed him and he said to me, "You know I am getting colder, colder all the time." I interpreted that to mean that he was telling me that he was going to die soon. I said to him, "Brother, I understand what you are trying to say to me." Then, I told him to rest a while and I will be back. I had read books about people's experiences about death and that it was not too unusual to have someone they know who had already passed over visit them.

I left the room because all of a sudden "the spirit of grief" seemed to envelop my emotions and I needed to be in a place where he could not see or hear me cry for a few minutes. I felt totally drained and I realized there was nothing more to do.

When I returned to his room I tried to get him to drink some water but he refused. I tried to tell him that he had to hang on and fight, that my husband would be home from Mexico by Monday or Tuesday and when he returned, we would take him to our home. But he just did not answer. I went home and returned later in the day with our daughter who had made him a huge card. When he saw it his eyes lit up. He apparently had never received a large card like that from anyone in his life.

Craig reached for Linda and he just held and kissed her like an uncle would do when he received something like that, for a long time. It was his way of saying "thank you" and showing her how special and meaningful it was to him to receive it. I could see that it was extremely special to him. (*Later I wondered if he just wanted her to know he loved her and wanted her to remember him.)*

That night I hated to leave his side, but I knew I must. It was hard for me to sleep that night and when I woke I felt a bit ill, realizing that I had no idea of what I might find in the morning. When I arrived he was worse and I was upset. I tried to contact the doctor and it took four hours. When I did, he agreed to transfer my brother back to the hospital.

At this point, I knew the time was near but I knew that he was not getting the right care in the convalescent hospital that would bring him out of it. By now he had caught pneumonia. Why hadn't that place heeded my pleas? The doctor told us that death would occur within a day or so and asked if we want him to have full life support system.

The doctor gave us some time to talk together as a family. Dad felt that " if" my brother could not have a quality of life and would need intensive care for a long period of time. Craig would not want to just lay there with no hope. So we agreed that no extreme measures would be taken to save his life and that we would release him into the hand of God. So, that is what we advised the doctor.

Eventually the cancer would take him anyway. The family left but I stayed on at the hospital. Somehow I just could not leave and I would go in and out of his room, watching and checking to see if he was all right.

I spent a little time in his room and I had an overwhelming sense that he was dying soon. His arm was lifted upward as though reaching for heaven. I prayed out loud hoping he might hear my prayer for his total healing, be it here or heaven. I prayed in the spirit. I sensed Craig heard me and knew what was happening although he was semi-comatose and unable to respond. I told him of our love for him, about God's love for him, and all the things I wish I could have said to him the first day we brought him home.

I sang a few Christian songs I loved to him, like Amazing Grace, and In the Garden and then told him I had to check on our daughter and I would be back in a few minutes. He looked like he was in perfect peace and his breathing was very shallow. I let the nurse know and then I went to be with our daughter in the waiting room. The nurse came out and notified me that he had passed on and she checked his vital signs and asked me if I needed any help. I told her that I had to call my parents and let them know he was gone. She let me use the hospital telephone in the nurse's station, which I deeply appreciated.

When I called them, Dad did not tell me that he was going to come to the hospital. I felt a bit shaky so I called our Pastor who met me at my car and followed Linda and me home. Shortly after, there was a knock at the door and it was Daddy. My husband was in Mexico. Dad stayed with us to be sure we were all right. We talked a little but only a few tears were shed because we both were trying to spare the other the emotion of it all. I could only imagine how Mother felt, my Aunt Vera was with her, I guess Dad thought I should not be alone, knowing the many emotional hours we had already put in watching over my brother. Dad was always so thoughtful and concerned where I was involved. I always appreciated his loving ways.

PART X

God's Infinite Love Heals All Grief and turns it into Joy!

CONCLUSION AND COMMENTS

My family has treated me as through I was fragile and weak. They never have understood the strength God has done within or what He has done in my life. His strength led me many times when I felt weak. Some things I had to face nearly paralyzed me with fear. Possibly I never really took time to share in depth with any of them because of my inability to put into verbal words what was in my heart. A few times I tried to reach out, but they were not ready to hear what I had to share. A few times I tried to put my faith and trust in God into words they implied I was some kind of fanatic. When I was asked to say table grace, it was too long for them and I was ridiculed. Eventually, I chose to not say it and remain silent. I am the oldest of three children in our family but often treated like the youngest. I never understood why?

I have been with most of those who have died, and I have handled their affairs, their funerals, etc. and I have felt that my family viewed me in a distorted way rather than who I really am. *Jesus has been and will always be my all in all,* He does come first in my life…

My brother Craig died eight days after Mother's birthday. One day I said, "Craig you know Mother's birthday will be here in a few days." Immediately he responded, "Sis, will you go out and purchase a nice bracelet for me to give to her." He wanted her to have something just from him. Again his thoughtfulness was so like our Dads.

Mother told me that those last days she had had several good talks with Craig. That really made it all worthwhile. I am sure she made him aware that she really loved him dearly. He told her he was all right and he loved her. He had been in places, seen things, met many people in his life and it was a full life and he had no regrets. It was his way of telling her how much he loved and still had missed her those years. His way of saying to her, "Mom, it's o.k!" I am sure that those times together filled a void in both their hearts and it was some thing they both longed for, for many years.

Dad has been diagnosed with terminal cancer about seven years before. He had been given three (3) months to live. His determination, courage, personal faith and trust in his medical team along with prayers offered in his behalf overruled the original diagnosis.

One day I heard Dad talking to Craig about his condition in his personal attempt to help Craig deal with his condition. Knowing Dad he probably gave him some positive reinforcement regarding science that was now available ultimately giving him some hope.

When Craig did pass away it left me feeling empty inside for a while. The purpose and goal of my life had finally been satisfied and fulfilled. In a sense I almost wanted to die too. Why hadn't God intervened and healed him sooner? I had a many questions. My faith seemed to waiver a bit as I grieved the loss. It seemed as though the Lord had moved so miraculously up to a point and we were in His perfect will. Now strangely enough I wanted to question the outcome of God's plan for us! Why had He refused to answer this prayer. What had I done wrong? I felt a little depressed for a few weeks. It was disappointing to not be able to take Craig "home" for just a little while and care for him. Of course God knew what all that would entail and the strain it would have put on our family, yet all of us were so willing to do it.

What an incredible year! Before this so many deaths already!! (1) My dearest and closest aunt Marion passed over September 3, 1979. After that within a short time one of my dearest friends (Mary Reinhart) passed away with a brain tumor. My uncle Gus went with me to her funeral. (2) In February on our anniversary, Marion's husband, Gus died very unexpectedly. *My aunt and uncle were like parents to me and left me everything they had in their will.. If they had not gifted me, we never would have had enough money to go and bring my brother home. I am eternally grateful for their love and devotion, but I would have never wanted them to die if it would have been my decision.*

(3)In April my husband's father, Harmon Norris in Roseboro, North Carolina died.

(4) In July my uncle Bob Julian (in his fifties) in Arizona was another surprising blow to the family. Now,

(5) on August 28, 1980 my dear brother died at age 42.

God's timing provided the finances for travel to the many funerals and hospital visits that took place. It would have been a financial burden for us because Richard was not able to work for over a year. It was impossible to carry on our own business under the stress of always having to be somewhere else so often. It was hard on our daughter having to miss so much school during the year and the emotional stress for a youngster.

If I hadn't received a gift of inheritance from my precious aunt and uncle, we probably never could have afforded doing all that we had to do on behalf of my brother and reconciliation with my parents. As much as I still appreciate their gift, I would give anything to have enjoyed them in my life all of these years.

In September 1980 my grandmother celebrated her ninety-third birthday. That day we had a little party at my parent's home. We were sitting out in the patio and uncle Milton said to me, "You know I am going to die before Mother?" I was taken back by his statement and in disbelief replied, "Oh No." I could not believe my ears. As I thought about it later I wondered if his own personal grief seeing the condition Craig was in and he was riddled with guilt and sadness. He lost his reason for living and

(6) Milton (professionally known as Michael Darren) died on October 9, 1980.

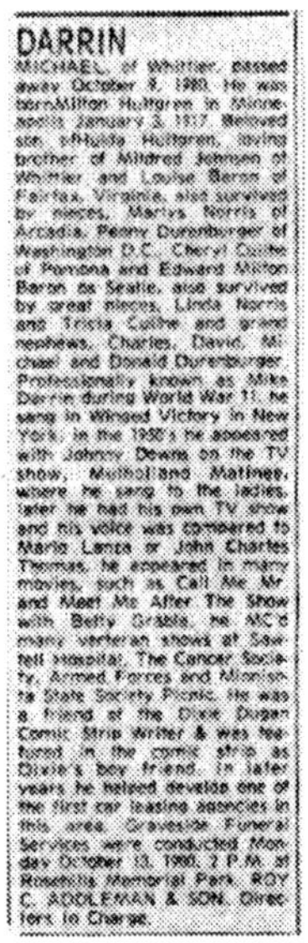

DARRIN

MICHAEL, of Whittier, passed away October 9, 1980. He was born Milton Hultgren in Minneapolis January 3, 1917. Beloved son of Hulda Hultgren, loving brother of Mildred Johnson of Whittier and Louise Baron of Fairfax, Virginia, also survived by nieces, Marys Norris of Arcadia, Penny Durenberger of Washington D.C., Cheryl Cuthe of Pomona and Edward Milton Baron of Seattle, also survived by great nieces, Linda Norris and Trisha Cuthe and grand nephews, Charles, David, Michael and Donald Durenberger. Professionally known as Mike Darrin during World War 11, he sang in Winged Victory in New York. In the 1950's he appeared with Johnny Downs on the TV show, Mulholland Matinee, where he sang to the ladies, later he had his own TV show and his voice was compared to Mario Lanza or John Charles Thomas. He appeared in many movies, such as Call Me Mr. and Meet Me After The Show with Betty Grable. He MC'd many veteran shows at Sawtelle Hospital, The Cancer Society, Armed Forces and Minnesota State Society Picnic. He was a friend of the Dixie Dugan Comic Strip Writer & was featured in the comic strip as Dixie's boy friend. In later years he helped develop one of the first car leasing agencies in this area. Graveside Funeral Services were conducted Monday October 13, 1980, 2 P.M. at Rosehills Memorial Park. ROY C. ADDLEMAN & SON, Directors in Charge.

I don't think he forgave himself for introducing our family to the Dahlbergs. No one ever accused him of anything that I am aware of.

He was a sensitive man and I can't help thinking that it bothered him a lot. If there was anything to forgive, he was forgiven years ago by all of us.

It is always so very hard to forgive ourselves for things that happen if we believe we are at all to blame. Some things we just have no control over and are innocent even with partial participation.

Gilda's determination was unbelievable and nothing was going to stand in her way of getting what she wanted.

We all would like a world where kindness and goodness prevail and relationships are honest and fair. Our family was like that along with always having a spirit of love and forgiveness.

(Years ago preachers taught little about believers having authority or power of God provided to us by God to use to ward off the satanic influences in this world. In His timetable, God was able to use us as his vessels to accomplish what He wanted to do. Years prior we did not know how use spiritual warfare against His foe that destroys families such as ours.)

Our first Christmas without family was full of sadness for us all. Our family dwindled down now. Each person had held a special significant place in our heart and lives. Now they were gone.

DAD'S CANCER RETURNS IN 1984

Dad's cancer returned and I was taking him for chemotherapy every few weeks. It was all that could be done and the cancer was taking hold again. The doctor recommended having a feeding tube put in his stomach as he could not swallow without gagging. He could die from malnutrition, which is a horrible painful death. It was an awesome decision but he knew that he was getting weaker and weaker. He decided to have the surgery on his birthday April 23, 1985.

Daddy was very quiet and personal about his own faith in God. We rarely talked and I was unable to share my faith and beliefs with him. The night before his surgery he beckoned my husband Richard and me to come closer to his bed and then he said, "Now, please say a little prayer." In that prayer, I prayed recommitting Dad into the hand of God and professing Jesus Christ as his personal Savior. I was so surprised that those are the only words I could think of saying. This was the first time Daddy had ever requested me to pray for him, even though I wanted to many times in the past. But I remained silent and quiet praying for him in my own "prayer closet" and never saying much about the fact I was praying for him at all. But I think he knew!

When Dad came home from the hospital after the surgery I stayed with my parents for those next few months, leaving my husband and daughter to tend for themselves. My dad felt much more comfortable having me take care of his needs. It amazed me that he let me! I had a sense that he fully trusted everything that I had to do for him. Sometimes I think that bothered Mother, but Dad knew Mother better than I did and he did not want her to get over-tired and worn out caring for him.

I learned to give breathing treatments, empty and count the urine, feed him every three hours through the feeding tub, and do personal things for him. I never dreamed he would ever let me do anything. When he wanted me he would buzz me in the middle of the night. He told me, "Maybe You missed your calling" meaning that maybe I should have been a nurse. He continually expressed deep appreciation for whatever I did. I really loved being able to do whatever I could for him.

This was the first time in my life, I felt so honored to have been able to do anything. I adored my dad and even though we never saw eye to eye on some things, I understood and respected his way of thinking and living.

One night, he had acute pains that he had never had before. He began to hallucinate and talk about strange things. It was time for his feeding and I had to feed him and without any warning, he just yanked out his feeding tube. He was rather delirious. I recognized similarities I remembered happening with my brother and I gasped in unbelief it was happening again. I immediately called the RN service. They came quickly and called the ambulance and Dad was taken to emergency. They tried to reinsert the tube but without success. I recall his painful scream and it tore at my heart.

This began three weeks of constant decline. He was given as much morphine as anyone can have in the hospital, but it never seemed to relieve all his pain and discomfort. Before he went into the hospital, he asked me to promise I would not leave him alone and I didn't unless someone else was there to sit with him. I think he knew he was dying and he had confidence he could lean on me and I would *not* fall apart. That really made me feel appreciated for the person I had become in Christ.

By the end of the third week I was not only exhausted but also frustrated because Dad who had never moaned and groaned in his life and now he was continuously doing it. I was helpless to change anything even though I kept asking for more morphine without any results. My husband sensed I was about to break down and stayed all night with me holding my dad's hand, so I could rest.

The first rays of sunlight began to fill the room. Morning approached and I sensed if I did not get out of there I would have an emotional break down right in Dad's room. So I told my Dad, I had to leave for a while. I told him that someone would be there to see him later in the morning. I wasn't sure he heard me but I told him anyhow.

I just could not stand him being in so much pain anymore and if I did not see him later in the day, I 'd see him in heaven. I was going home to rest a day and get hold of my emotions and told him why I was leaving.. I imagined his eye twitching as though he heard me. Dad would have wanted me to leave and I did. A few hours after arriving home the telephone rang. My sister called. My aunt Vera, Mother and Cheryl had gone to the hospital and Dad had died. They asked me if I wanted to go there and say goodbye. I felt I had already done that before I left. I felt no one really understood but I knew Dad, God and I knew everything was all right. This was the first time since he first was diagnosed with cancer, I was willing to 'let him go'.

(Hospice Program advises that when it is time, we need to give our loved one permission to leave us and go to heaven. I guess telling Dad if I didn't see him tomorrow, I would see him in heaven indicated to him that I realized it was near his time and I could handle it.)

Seeing someone you love in so much pain, helps a person to "release him or her into the hand of God". Maybe that is why God allows it!!!

Dad represented strength to me, I felt his power and security as long as he was living. His illness and weakness never diminished it.. I wish all children could enjoy the kind of strength and security we enjoyed. He was a gentle quiet man, but strong and mighty in ways other than physical. We were so privileged to have had the parents God gave us. In spite of it all, both of our parents taught us much about life in their personal suffering.

Surviving was truly evidenced by the strong and mighty faith that they had developed from childhood.. I can only hope that a tiny bit of all that they represented will be passed on to our future generations. It was God's grace and mercy that sustained all of us though out this tragedy…and reunited us in the end… God miraculously removed our mountain!

It was always amazing to me that my parents never blamed God. They never expressed any anger at Him because things did not turn out their way. They taught us to respect and honor the Lord in our lives and because of this teaching .....we have been blessed.

Mother is gone now too. She was a courageous soul to the very end. The following is what I wrote for her "Graduation Service".

TRIBUTE TO MOTHER
God Promises to turn our Grief into Joy!

It was an awesome experience to see our mother's faith and trust in God in the final weeks of her life. Her wisdom and courage were profound and her ability to accept what was happening to her body incredible.

Mother decided not to proceed with the dialysis treatments because they were not working properly. The nurse advised her that this would end her life. Going to the dialysis treatments, getting in and out of the car and just laying there for three and a half hours became increasingly tiring, exhausting her strength and distressing her. Knowing Mother, you know that she never complained.. Mother had a way of making the "best" out of every situation. She was always grateful and positive and delightfully progressive for her age.

The last month began with a little activity, which slowly regressed to little or nothing physically. Her mind remained in tact and she was able to request and communicate what she wanted or needed.

During the day and every night at bedtime we gave one another hugs, kisses and told each other we loved one another. Every night we prayed together.

One thing that was especially a blessing to both of us was remembering events that happened years ago. God seemed to cause me to remember things Mother did for me as a child that I appreciated. So, I told her how much it meant to me then and now. It seemed to bring her great delight to know that her "mothering" was remembered and appreciated.

As the time of her passing grew closer, a deeper dimension to our relationship seemed to develop.. A bonding and a love that far surpassed anything I had known as an adult. In fact, it was the love I actually felt as a child and it was a wonderful feeling. An added blessing from God!

The night before Mother passed over as I watched over her during the night. Six or seven times she would raise her hand as though she were about to take someone's hand or possibly she was Praising God! I would go to her and whisper in her ear that I loved her, kiss her and ask her. "Was she praising God? Are you about to take the Angels' hand and slip away to heaven? Was she praying? Did she see the Lord waiting in the Light across the bridge? The last time I told her.. I knew that time was getting closer and when she wanted to go, it was all right.. We would all be all right. She was a courageous human being. And I thanked her! Up until this time, mother showed some sort of response to whatever was said to her.

In the morning, the bathing nurse came and she indicated that the time was very close. Mother waited until my sister Cheryl called after work. I went in and told her Cheryl said she loved her and was concerned about how she was doing. It was not five minutes and Mother took her two last breaths. She was gone—now, gone to her eternal home.

Mother did not only teach me how to live. But so much more…right to the very end. I am an eternally grateful daughter.

I could not write this book while our parents were both alive because I did not want to open up wounds that appeared to have been healed to some degree when my brother, Craig was brought home and then died. As I write it now, I prayed that it would ..in its end bring some honor and glory to God for the miracle of reconciliation He so graciously gave to us.

"TO GOD BE THE GLORY FOR ALL HE HAS DONE"…

MISCELLANEOUS PAPERS RELATING OUR STORY

THIS IS A LETTER DADDY WROTE................
TO: State of Florida Courts
Miami, Florida

To whom it may concern:

This letter is written to state our position as natural parents of Craig Marvin Johnsen as to the petition for adoption, which have been filed in. ...Etc. by Bror and Gilda Dahlberg *without our knowledge or consent.* We protest such action and hope in this letter to give you the true picture of what has transpired since 1944 and the circumstances, which have led to the present situation.

In July 1944 we were living in Minneapolis, Minnesota and had lived there all of our lives. The Dahlbergs had a summer home on an island in Rainy Lake on the North boundary of the state and want there to spend the summer. With them came Mrs. Johnsen's brother Milton who drove to Minneapolis to visit his family and brought an invitation from the Dahlbergs to invite his niece and nephew, namely Craig and his sister Marlys to come back with him and spend a few weeks at the lake.

We consented to this and Craig and Marlys spent some weeks at the lake and Marlys came home by bus alone. Soon after Marlys arrival home, we were deluged with phone calls, telegrams, and letters requesting that we allow Craig to accompany his uncle and the Dahlbergs to California for the winter only and he would be brought home in the spring. They did not bring him home as was promised, Gilda had taken off with Craig to California without our permission or knowledge.

Upon our constant plea by all means of communication to bring Craig home, the Dahlbergs suggested instead that we visit them in California. We could get no action so Mrs. Johnsen did go to California with Marlys and Craig's new sister born January 1945. Cheryl. It being impossible for Mr. Johnsen (myself) to leave his employment.

They stayed seven weeks or so and returned to Minneapolis and Craig remained in California upon the plea we should not interrupt

Craig School year and also the country was experiencing a polio epidemic and

California was the least affected we were told. Again we were promised Craig would be home for sure in the next summer.

The summer of 1946 presented the same problem as the previous summer and the Dahlbergs refused to bring Craig home despite our pleas. The fall of 1946 the Dahlbergs hired Mrs. Johnsen's sister and her husband as household help in their home in California and I, Craig's father made the trip with them to California to visit Craig and with intent to bring him home. During the time of my visit I was prevailed upon to let Craig stay another winter, and with two uncles and an aunt in the Dahlberg household I felt he would be safe and agreed with the understanding this was the last.

Mr. Dahlbergs valet brought Craig home in the summer of 1947. After a time Mrs. Dahlberg came over to our home and wanted Craig to go with her again We refused to allow it.

Mrs. Dahlberg suggested that she, Craig and his little sister and a neighbor girl go with her in her limousine.... to get some ice cream. A block down she told the neighbor girl and Craigs little sister to get out and they took off for the lake home some 350 miles from Minneapolis. In this she was aided and abetted by the valet, Doc by name and presumably the hired driver.

Upon being informed of this at my work, I left immediately for the lake home arriving the next morning after an all night drive. I contacted the Sheriff in International Falls, Minnesota, explained my problem and was told he could do nothing until a complaint was filed at the source of the crime being Minneapolis.

I left notice with him that if I was not back by an specified time to look for me on the Dahlberg's Island we got Craig in the boat and started back to shore. At the last possible moment Mrs. Dahlberg threw herself into the boat. We proceeded toward shore but Mrs. Dahlberg created such a hazard by language and throwing herself about that we had to return to the island rather than continue to endanger our lives.

Mr. Dahlberg was due on the island shortly, so thinking I could reason with him, I dismissed my boat with instructions to notify the sheriff of our predicament. Mr. Dahlberg arrived shortly, saw the error of the situation and set Craig and I ashore in one of his boats.

Mrs. Dahlberg came to Minneapolis soon after with tearful protestations that she meant no harm and entreated us to let the children enjoy summer at the lake. Craig, Marlys and a neighbor child went to the lake as her guests and we thought everything would now be all right. Mr. Dahlberg assured me he personally would see that Mrs. Dahlberg behaved. It was not to be.

Marlys and the neighbor child arrived home on a bus with no notice to us and we found that Mrs. Dahlberg had taken Craig to California with her repeating her past offense of taking him without our consent or knowledge. All our pleas were to no avail. We finally decided the only way left was to go and get Craig.

Craig's mother left for California shortly before Christmas. Several days after she left I received in the mail a Petition for Guardianship, which had been filed by the Dahlbergs in the Los Angeles California courts without our knowledge or consent. Craig's mother was not well received by the Dahlbergs and upon one occasion physically attacked and struck by Mrs. Dahlberg.

Mr. Dahlberg on Christmas Eve, relented to the event that Craig and his mother were allowed to go to church together accompanied by a bodyguard. Craig's Mother instructed the bodyguard to drive to her uncle's church and dismissed him. After church they left for his home and the chauffer followed them.

He became violent, saying he had instructions not to let them go anyplace, cut the phone wires but a member of the family got a call through first and the police arrived. The Dahlbergs were called and arrived with attorney *(Sam Yorty)* Mrs. Johnsen had retained. The Dahlbergs found they had no legal standing and the police dismissed all.

The Dahlbergs returned and continued the harassment tactics a good share of the night, knocking on doors and windows and shouting threats. On being notified of all this I Craig's father flew there the next day.

The Dahlbergs caused to be issued a restraining order preventing us from leaving California, we were told later, but we were never served with it and went back to Minneapolis.

We were instantly and constantly deluged with all types of pressure by phone, mail, telegram and the visit to our home of prominent attorney, Joseph Scott to plead with us to let Craig go to California again.

I was a Postal employee and an attempt was made to get me fired without my knowledge. This move was not successful. Although we were never contacted by these people we found the Dahlbergs had made advances to the Mayor of Minneapolis, the Pastor of our church and others to convince us or force us, I don't know which, to give in to the Dahlberg demands.

After a month and a half of this we went to Chicago to see the Dahlbergs and a final solution was reached, we thought. Mr. Dahlberg offered me a job with his firm, The Celotex Corp., in the Los Angles office and we were all to move to California. This was agreed to and Craig was to re enter the school he had been in before and to spend his free weekends at home and with the Dahlbergs alternately.

I resigned my position in the Postal Service and the move was made in 1948. This worked to a degree until the summer of 1949 with the Dahlbergs becoming increasingly difficult as Craig enjoyed so much being at home.

The break came on a weekend Craig was spending home when they insisted Craig be returned to school many hours ahead of the scheduled time which we had determined at the school. We decided then that there was no way to get along with the Dahlbergs except on their terms, so we decided to call everything off and live our own lives as a family.

Three or four days later a deputy came to our home with a signed court order, ordering us to surrender Craig to him for return to the school. Seeing no alternative but to comply with the law, we allowed the deputy to return Craig to the school.

Immediately Mrs. Dahlberg seized him and she left for parts unknown. All legal aspects of our problem were returned over to our attorney. Nothing was accomplished to our knowledge until the petition for guardianship of December 1949 was filed.

In the meantime I was discharged from the Celotex Corp on the pretext they were cutting the sales force. The opposite was true. In the next few days the Celotex Corp hired several additional salesmen in the Los Angles area.

The guardianship of December 1949 we agreed to by Craig's mother and myself for several reasons. In view of all that had gone before we felt a court proceeding could only breed more bitterness and for Craig's sake we wished to avoid that.

The court set up specific rights of visitation for us and we felt the Dahlbergs would recognize that as they had not recognized their verbal promises in the past.

Under the terms of the guardianship the situation did not improve. We appealed to all concerned and Craig made his first and last visit home in April of 1950. Under the terms Craig was to come home one day per month, five days in June and five days in September.

After the April 1950 visit the Dahlbergs left the State of California and we have failed to find them and knew not where they were until we received this petition for Adoption.

Our attorney filed a contempt action for failure to live up to the terms of guardianship but was unable to locate the Dahlbergs to serve them. We have written Craig constantly, sent him gifts and was only able to address them through the Celotex Corp. Chicago. C/o Bror Dahlberg. We have no knowledge that he ever received these letters and gifts and those that were acknowledged were by notes so stilted and precise that we felt that they did not reflect a boy of Craig's age might say. By Marvin J. Johnsen 2/23/54

This is the little girl who was put out of the car when Craig was kidnapped!

NOTARIZED AFFIDAVITS READ AS FOLLOWS: Nancy's Letter

During the summer of 1947, one day I was over to the Johnsen home at 2315 Garfield Ave So, Minneapolis, Minnesota and when I got there, Mrs. Marvin Johnsen, Mrs. Gilda Dahlberg, Marlys Johnsen, Craig Johnsen, Cheryl Johnsen were in the home.

Mrs. Gilda Dahlberg had asked Craig if he wanted to go for a ride, and he didn't want to go, she kept asking and he finally said he would if someone would go with him. In the meantime Mrs. Marvin Johnsen had sent Marlys to the store for some things for lunch, to which Mrs. Dahlberg said she would have some. Mrs. Johnsen was in the kitchen preparing coffee and sandwiches when Mrs. Dahlberg said she was going to take Craig, Cheryl and myself (Nancy Sandell) for a little ride while Millie was getting lunch ready.

Mrs. Dahlberg and the three of us (Craig, Cheryl and myself) went out to the large green limosine with Illinois license plates and had a chauffeur driving it. And a little girl name of Bonnie Lee related to the Dahlbergs. Mrs. Dahlberg had flown in to Minneapolis and said the chauffeur had driven down from Chicago.

We rode to the corner of Franklin and Garfield, a litter over a block away and stopped. Mrs. Dahlberg asked me to get out of the car and handed Cheryl to me, and Craig wanted to get out but she would not let him so he began to cry. She closed the door and drove off with Craig, Bonnie Lee, and the Chauffeur and left us standing there. We ran home to Mrs. Johnsen's and told her what happened to Craig and she cried and cried as did Marlys. Marlys and I looked around the neighborhood for Craig but could not find him.

In talking it over the Johnsen's decided that she took him to their summer home known as Red Crest at International Falls, Minnesota on the Canadian border. Then Mr. Johnsen and two others went to International Falls to get Craig and he brought him back a few days later. Signed and Notarized... Nancy Sandell

****

Prepared as "proof of the kidnapping" attempt by Gilda Dahlberg

CATHERINE'S NOTARIZED AFFIDAVIT READS:

I was at the home of Mr. And Mrs. Marvin Johnsen when Mrs. Gilda Dahlberg was prevailing upon Craig Johnsen to go up to Red Crest with her for a summer vacation or at least until Mr. And Mrs. Johnsen went up to International Falls for a Mail Carriers Convention to which I believe Mr. Johnsen was a delegate. All this was taking place after Mr. Johnsen had gone to International Falls to get Craig and bring him home after Mrs. Dahlberg has spirited him away after supposedly taking him for a ride while Mrs. Johnsen was preparing lunch.

Craig did not want to go, but Mrs. Dahlberg had been very nice to the Johnsen's and apologized for her actions and kept after Craig to go to Red Crest with her. Craig finally said he would go if his sister Marlys could go with him, but Marlys wanted me to go and Mrs.

Dahlberg agreed to this, and promised to bring Craig back home to his parents or that he would go home with his parents after the convention at International Falls.

After a few days at Red Crest, Marlys told Mrs. Dahlberg that her parents were coming to International Falls for the convention. Then Mr. And Mrs. Dahlberg, Marlys, Craig and I immediately went over to the boys camp to see if they could take Craig for a while and what he would need. We then returned to Red Crest and Mrs. Dahlberg prepared Craig's things and took him right back to the camp all in the same day. This was the only time Marlys and I saw Craig all the time we were on the island

Except when we were at a few meals together. Mrs. Dahlberg kept giving us excuses and sending us on errands to keep us away from seeing Craig.

A few days later Marlys, her aunt Marion and uncle Gus and I went to International Falls to pick up Mr. And Mrs. Johnsen at the Rex Hotel, where they were at this convention and they came to the island for the evening meal. This was on Thursday, because the Cruiser "Gilda" caught on fire that evening. We got off the boat and went to the cottage where aunt Marion was staying when Mrs Johnsen asked how Craig was and we said fine. When Mrs. Johnsen got into the cottage and asked where Craig was, Marion told her Mrs. Dahlberg had sent him off to camp on another island. Mrs. Johnsen cried and cried. Mrs. Dahlberg came down from the main house and acted very friendly towards her to get her to stop crying, inviting the Johnsens up to the main house for dinner. Mrs. Johnsen wanted to see Craig, but he had gone on an extended boat trip; with the boys at the camp, so she didn't see him all the time she was there.

At the main house they had dinner and discussed all the wonderful things that they were going to do for the Johnsens and Craig. Then Mr. And Mrs. Dahlberg and Mr. And Mrs. Johnsen went into the living room to talk, and every time I or Marlys entered the living room we were told to leave and not permitted to hear what was going on or said.

Mrs. Dahlberg promised that as soon as Craig was back from camp she would bring him home to the Johnsens. But I never saw Craig since the time Mrs. Dahlberg took him to camp because when he did get back she took him direct to California instead of to his parents as promised. Signed and Notarized Catherine Sandell

THE END
-0-0-

SUNDAY NEWS, JANUARY 18, 1948

A Self-Made Millionaire

The Home That Craig Left

An intimate study of the Bror Dahlbergs' modernistic Beverly Hills bungalow. Note combination indoor-outdoor living room, with Mrs. Dahlberg in outdoor section next edge of pool. Craig used to live here.

Celotex King Dahlberg Fights to Heap Luxury On Johnsen Youngster

By JESS STEARN

WHEN Bror Dahlberg was a small boy his mother told him that you never get anything for nothing and if you want to succeed in this world you have to give of yourself until there is nothing left to give.

This may be why Bror is one of the country's richest men today, a captain of industry, chairman of the fabulous Celotex Corp., guiding genius of a dozen other corporations. And it also may be why he has had so much trouble for so many years.

Wherever Bror is, things have a way of happening. And in Hollywood, where Bror lives and where virtually every big shot is known as dynamic, they are at a loss for a word for Bror—except, of course, that he is superdynamic and maybe super-super; surely high praise for anyone not in movies.

At 67, an age when most millionaires are at least talking of retiring, the chunky, vital Bror is busy with new plans and new problems. One plan calls for dream homes for millions of young Americans; one problem—strictly personal—calls for straightening out his own dream home, presently jeopardized by loss of a child he loved as his own.

Dahlberg, for all his vitality, has had no children of his own in the course of two interesting marriages, and this may be why he is waging so intense a fight for 10-year-old Craig Johnsen, the Minneapolis mailman's son he and Mrs. Dahlberg have had for the last five years.

Right now, the Johnsens have the boy, having carried him away from a life of luxury on Christmas Day, but the Dahlbergs hope to have him back soon. A custody hearing is already down on the docket, but since the Johnsens aren't in California, the probabilities are the hearing will be put off until the boy is produced by his parents.

The Johnsens, having agreed to let the boy go to California for his health, apparently were content to let the Dahlbergs keep him, educate him, spend their money on him—until recently when Bror filed a petition to legalize his guardianship over Craig.

Sought to Provide A Legal Basis.

The way Dahlberg tells it, he had not planned to adopt the boy or otherwise invalidate the parents' natural rights, but had thought it wise to provide some legal basis for helping the boy in the future.

He acted, he says, with the consent of the mother, and was therefore surprised when she descended on the Dahlberg dream house with an arsenal of fire and brimstone shortly before the holidays.

There was a series of heated talks, ending in fisticuffs on Christmas Eve when Mrs. Johnsen asserts that Mrs. Dahlberg pushed her about in the course of the discussions.

At any rate, Mrs. Johnsen managed to get out of the Dahlberg house with Craig and took refuge in the nearby home of her uncle, Dr. George Holtgren, a professor at the University of California at Los Angeles.

The Dahlbergs' loyal chauffeur trailed mother and son into the Holtgren home and hung around until the cops were called to throw him out. Later that evening the Dahlbergs called, but the cops were again summoned and the Dahlbergs left.

Then, the following morning, on advice of counsel Sam Yorty, Mrs. Johnsen got out of town with Craig, only a few hours before the Dahlbergs got a restraining order which would have kept the boy from being removed from California until the question of guardianship was settled.

At present, Dahlberg's wife, Gilda, years younger than he and almost as energetic, is taking the boy's loss even harder than her husband. It was Gilda who first persuaded the Johnsens to let her take the frail boy away from the rigorous Minnesota climate.

At that time, Craig was a sickly child of 5. With his parents, Mr. and Mrs. Marvin Johnsen, and a sister he had been visiting the Dahlbergs' Summer place at Red-crest Island, Ranier, Minnesota, not far from where Bror began his meteoric career.

Ordinarily the Dahlbergs and the Johnsens would hardly meet in a social way. However, the Dahlbergs, particularly Gilda, have always been interested in young people and their careers and one of Gilda's protégés at the time was one Milton Hultgren, who was trying to make a singer of himself. Milton, who happens to be Mrs. Johnsen's brother, had arranged for the Johnsens' visit.

Gilda, childless in two marriages, was captivated by Craig, and immediately undertook to do something for him. She took him to a Minneapolis doctor, who reported, she says, that the child might not survive unless he were taken to a milder climate.

The Johnsens, confronted with this diagnosis, agreed to let the boy go off with Gilda and Bror. In California, Craig responded to the sunshine and the best care that money could buy. He was sent off to exclusive Chadwicke School, where he rubbed elbows with millionaires' sons and learned what it's like to have everything he wanted.

Meanwhile, the Dahlbergs' fondness for Craig led to a sympathetic interest in other members of the family. Bror offered to find a job in Southern California for Craig's father, but the veteran mail carrier doubted the job's stability and stayed on in Minnesota.

As the years passed, several reunions were arranged for Craig and his family, Mrs. Johnsen being the Dahlbergs' house guest a number of times and the boy occasionally getting to Minnesota. Last Summer, 12-year-old Marlys, the older of Craig's two sisters, spent a couple of weeks at the Dahlbergs' Minnesota lodge, and the welcome mat has always been out for other Johnsens.

Even now the Dahlbergs say they feel no particular animosity toward the elder Johnsens. They just want to get Craig back and give him the care they think he needs.

* * *

BROR is what is commonly known as a self-made man, and it may be significant that he is trying to spare Craig the same designation. He was 11, only a year older than Craig is now, when he came to this country from Sweden, the second oldest of a brood of five. Bror attributes his success to his mother, who kept her children alive and healthy and filled them with an overwhelming desire to get ahead.

Bror's father didn't live long and the kids all had to hustle. They lived on the outskirts of Minneapolis, where rent was cheap, and, at 14, Bror had begun to run a rope elevator for the Northern Pacific Railroad.

He walked 11 miles each way and collected $15 a month for 12 hours a day. This, he tells News correspondent Florabel Muir, taught him that it didn't pay to be poor and he looked about for a way out.

A second-hand Pitman shorthand book which he bought for a nickel proved to be the key to success. He taught himself shorthand and typing when he wasn't running the elevator. Finally, he was efficient enough to get a stenographer's job and worked his way up through the various departments of the railroad and its lumbering business, every now and then drawing a nod of approval from head man James J. Hill.

Quit Railroading to Enter Lumber Business.

Despite this progress, Bror saw that it would take him much longer than he wanted to take to get Hill's job; so he quit the railroad and went into the lumber business for himself. Eventually this led to Celotex.

"I saw," he recalls, "that lumbering stood a good chance of running out in this country and I began experimenting with something that would take the place of lumber.

"I wanted some waste product that wasn't worth anything to anybody. I first thought of straw, but I soon found out that straw was worth a lot to the farmer because he could use it for insulation for his house and barns, bedding for his stock and as mulch for the soil.

"Then I came across bagasse (a French word meaning refuse), which is the sugar cane stalk after everything of value has been removed. This stuff was no good for mulch because it would not disintegrate in the soil but remained a soggy mass.

"This was the thing I had been looking for and in 1920 I started my first mill in Marrero, near New Orleans, to manufacture celotex out of bagasse. Now I have 10 mills in different parts of the world. One is in Stonebridge Park near London, one in Los Angeles, one in Sweden, one in New Jersey."

From bagasse it was a short step for Dahlberg to buy up sugar fields and grow his own bagasse. He [illegible] [illegible] sugar [illegible]

SUNDAY NEWS, JANUARY 18, 1948

And a 10-Year-Old Boy

Principals

Here (A) is an exterior view of the hilltop house in which Bror and his wife Gilda (→) live alone since Mrs. Mildred Johnson carried off her son Craig (←), with whom she is shown here.

fields all over the world, the largest in a section of the Florida Everglades, which he has reclaimed with great perseverance.

Dahlberg, nothing if not thorough, began experimental work on sugar growing and imported cane sprouts, marrying the seeds and raising new kinds of cane.

He learned that the first sugar cane had been discovered in New Guinea. Traveling there with a pre-war expedition partly financed by the U. S. Government, he found a crude cane yielding 300 tons to the acre—compared to Cuban cane producing 17 to 20 tons per acre.

The New Guinea cane was transplanted, acclimated, crossed and recrossed with the most refined growths of cane; now Dahlberg cane yields 50 to 70 tons per acre of the finest sugar.

From sugar Dahlberg went into oil, and from celotex into cemesto, which he hopes will go a long way toward relieving the country's housing problem.

Sell Mansion to Live in Bungalow.

Bror already has built several houses of this material, a combination of celotex [illegible] and cement, which is compressed, hardened and then [illegible] off to any desired wall length.

Cemesto, according to Bror, will never wear out. He plans building thousands of cemesto houses when conditions permit—whenever that is.

The Dahlbergs recently sold their big mansion in Beverly Hills and now live in one of Bror's modernistic, streamlined bungalows on a bluff overlooking the city. There is a swimming pool, a wonderful view, and no servant problem, Mrs. Dahlberg says, because the house is small.

"You should live in such a small house," our Miss Muir writes. "They have four bedrooms, multitudinous baths, and yards of patios."

Mrs. Dahlberg is considered extremely social for Hollywood and has become celebrated for her parties in a community where it is distinctive not to give them or go to them. She also sponsors little theatre groups and helps struggling young artists, such as Milton Lindgren, whenever she is in the mood.

Her interest in the theatre may well go back to her own fling at the stage 20 years ago, when, as Gilda Kreegan (nee Kriegers), she had the lead in the Broadway musical, "Little Jessie James." In those days she was a diminutive, dark-eyed brunette, pleasingly slim, and the years have wrought no great change. She is still pleasing.

The Dahlbergs have been married nearly 16 years, and in that time there has been scarcely a rumble of discord. She insists [illegible] be [illegible] to like it.

They were married on May 16, 1932, less than a month after Dahlberg had won a divorce from beautiful, social-climbing Mary Alexander Dahlberg, on grounds of desertion. The marriage was also the second for Gilda, alternately known as Goldie at that phase in her career.

Gilda had been married to a business man named Bert Lichtie, and got divorced after Lichtie ran out on her for another woman. Gilda was so upset by his defection at the time that she sued her rival for $100,000 worth of alienation of affections.

Earlier, evidently with no success, Gilda had frantically wired her rival, a wealthy widow:

"You have your baby. I have nothing in the world but my husband. Don't take him from me."

There was no response and later, in lieu of her husband, Gilda received an out-of-court settlement of $17,500.

Shortly after she became Mrs. Dahlberg, Gilda again found occasion to turn to the courts. This time she sued *Sir Eric Dutt*, a Hindu nabob, for $150,000, charging he had slandered her on two continents.

Gilda, who had known Sir Eric abroad, accused him of spreading word she was an adventuress and had roamed with men she had not taken time to marry.

Eventually the suit was settled out of court, with Sir Eric making a handsome apology, and Gilda accepting it in lieu of the 150 Gs.

* * *

IN the years to follow, Gilda became socially acceptable as wife of the celotex king and for her own many charms, though it usually turned out that she footed the bill for any large social entertainment with which she was connected.

One of these was the ill-starred Park Avenue Canteen, a wartime project in which Gilda had involved herself with Mrs. Hammond Tayloe, Mrs. Richard Washburn Child, Mrs. Thackaberry McAdoo, and others.

Through no fault of Gilda's, the Canteen came into bad odor after an investigation by the D.A.'s office into its fund-raising methods, and was shut down as it was getting ready to open.

Gilda, unaffected, wanted to patronize independently, using her husband's money if necessary, but her newfound Park Ave. pals, not accustomed to tangling with the law, took fright and melted away like snow.

Any wartime entertaining of service men by Gilda from this date was individual. An inspection of the era's social activity indicates that Gilda turned to entertaining such celebrities as Lady Mendl, who, with the possible exception of the Duchess of Windsor, is easily the world's most entertained person.

At this one entertainment for Lady Mendl, the distinguished guest was the Princess Margaret of Denmark, who by her democratic manner—the society reporters unanimous—delighted all present, Mrs. Dahlberg included.

The following day was a bright one on Mrs. Dahlberg's calendar. She was the envy of Park Ave. for bringing off this coup. It was almost up to the notable triumph scored by the first Mrs. Dahlberg when she brought a genuine, pre-abdication Spanish princess to her Chicago hacienda and had all of Windy City society challenging her to prove it.

Mary Alexander, not too fresh from Texas, had married Dahlberg in 1921 after making a considerable dent on the elite of the Chicago underworld.

Mary's name had been linked continuously with racketeer John Factor, and some suggested the friendship had been blessed by matrimony.

She had been snubbed for years, despite celotex, and was bitter about the whole thing when she hit on importing the Princess Marie de Bourbon of Spain as her house guest.

When unnerved socialites intimated the Princess was an impostor—she was openly called a "royal four flush"—Mrs. Dahlberg promptly obtained signed and sealed credentials from the Spanish Embassy in Washington, certifying her Royal Highness was a second cousin of King Alfonso (remember?), and that anybody should be proud to entertain a Bourbon.

Many of Chicago's elite pretended they didn't give a hang. But anonymous letters kept pouring in to the newspapers knocking the Princess and saying how the Dahlbergs were social upstarts and the Princess was only a circus stunt to get Mrs. Dahlberg's face on the society pages and help Bror unload some Florida property on which the Princess was to dedicate a church he had built. Bror was quick to deny this, saying he had no intention of selling any land.

Eventually, stung by the unkind comment, Mary blamed the anonymous letters on various Chicago social leaders, including Mrs. Potter Palmer Brown, and referred to the whole lot of them in one breath as "[illegible] society."

Of these, only Mrs. Brown saw fit to register indignation in a public way. Charging defamation of character, she brought suit against Mary for $200,000, but the suit never came off.

To establish further that she was as social as anybody, Mary, arbitrarily confident, entrusted the American Historical Society with the job of checking her blood lines, and induced Bror to give his antecedents a once-over, too.

After a year of sleuthing in the monasteries and graveyards of Europe, the obliging genealogists reported Mary descended from William the Conqueror, Robert Bruce, the Baron of Nova Scotia and the Viscount of Canada.

Dahlberg was not nearly as distinguished. The historical society could work him back only to 1626, connecting him to Jean Ericksson Dahlberg, a Swedish revenue collector, and inserting as only the noble [illegible], Count Erik Dahlberg, who led Swedish armies into Poland on a memorable occasion.

He Didn't Want to Pay Research Bill.

However, after Erik, Bror's line was lost sight of for 180 years. Being a hardheaded business man he was unable to understand how he could be traced to Count Dahlberg when there was no way of connecting him to the Count's immediate descendants.

Even promise of the Dahlberg coat-of-arms—a lion rampant—failed to banish Dahlberg's doubts, and he startled everybody concerned, including his wife, when he announced he was not going to pay the historical society's bill, which came to $1,700.

Eventually, the society sued, but before the case reached trial the Dahlbergs were divorced, both had remarried, and Mary was in another Chicago court trying to collect 140,000 back alimony from Bror.

After her divorce, in 1932, Mary married Bentley Chapin, a millionaire artist eight years younger than she. Dahlberg had stopped payments to Mary, claiming Chapin had enough for the two. When Mary held this to be irrelevant, Dahlberg tossed his bombshell.

Through lawyers, he charged Mary had no claim on him because they had never been really married, contending she had been legally bound to [illegible], since liquidated in gang warfare, when she said yes to him.

At this interesting juncture the case was removed from the courtroom to private chambers. Dahlberg's counsel subsequently consented to announce the suit had been settled for $2,500 and you could draw what conclusions you liked.

Some time later Mary went to Albuquerque, N. M., to live, and there she died in July, 1938. Whatever else she was, she was interesting, and she exerted tremendous influence on the money-maker. Even now, 10 years after her death, Dahlberg refuses to talk about her—and this is virtually the only subject he won't discuss.

Dahlbergs Gain Ground in Child Custody Row

Post-Advocate Los Angeles Bureau

Los Angeles Superior Judge William B. McKesson today overruled a demurrer of Marvin J. and Mildred Johnson of Alhambra, to a suit by multi-millionaire Bror Dahlberg, president of the Celotex Corporation over the custody of the Johnson 11-year-old son, Craig.

The jurist gave the Johnsons ten days to answer the Dahlberg complaint in which they claim they have spent $25,000 on the care and education of the boy during the past seven year. and $50,000 on the Johnson family.

Mrs. Dahlberg, in an affidavit, declared that Craig was under-nourished and anemic when she found him at the Dahlberg's home for under-privileged children in 1942.

She claimed that his life was saved by their bringing him to California.

Superior Judge Clarence M. Hanson on June 15 issued an injunction sought by the Dahlbergs to prevent the parents of their protege from removing him from the Chadwick School for Boys.

The Johnson demurrer contended the Dahlbergs did not have sufficient facts to constitute a cause of action, and declared that a prior agreement giving the Dahlbergs custody of the boy could not be recognized as a legal and conclusive contract because unfavorable circumstances required surrendering the child.

—Herald-Express Photo

DAHLBERG-JOHNSEN GUARDIAN FIGHT NEAR SETTLEMENT

Settlement of a bitter guardian fight over [illegible] Johnsen, 12, on whom Millionaire [illegible] rialist Bror Dahlberg has [illegible] was reported near today. [illegible] will continue in custody of the boy and share in a joint 1-year guardianship with the boy's parents, Marvin and Mildred Johnsen. [illegible] are pictured in court with daughters, Cheryl, 4, and Marliss, 15. [illegible]

DANIEL A. MACDONALD, M. D.
1035 E. FRANKLIN AVE.
MINNEAPOLIS 4, MINNESOTA

June 27, 1949

To Whom It May Concern:

Mr. and Mrs. E. L. Hultgren have been patients of mine since I brought Mrs. Marvin J. Johnson into the world. I have taken care of the family since then in different illnesses and brought the three children of Mr. and Mrs. Marvin J. Johnson into the world.

My records show attendance on these children at various times and among them treatment of Marlys in December 1941 for Impetigo and vaccinated two of the children in September 1942.

I have always felt that Mr. and Mrs. Hultgren and their children were of the finest in character and all other qualities which would make them good citizens. I attended the parents of Mr. E. L. Hultgren, the Rev. Andrew G. Hultgren, and wife. I also have had over these many years sisters and brothers of both Mr. Hultgren and his wife for patients.

I recommend highly all the relationships of these fine people for their sincerity, integrity and all that make good Christian people.

Daniel A. MacDonald M.D.

Daniel A. MacDonald, M. D.

Sworn to before a Notary in and for said Hennepin County this twenty seventh day of June 1949.

Ruth Parker

My commission expires Novenber 29th, 1954.

DENTAL CERTIFICATE

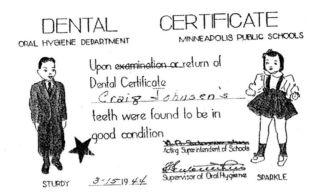

ORAL HYGIENE DEPARTMENT — MINNEAPOLIS PUBLIC SCHOOLS

Upon ~~examination or~~ return of Dental Certificate *Craig Johnsen's* teeth were found to be in good condition

Healthy Teeth

Acting Superintendent of Schools

Supervisor of Oral Hygiene

STURDY *3-15* 19*44* SPARKLE

174 (40M 7-43 V)

The Deaconess Hospital

1412 East 24th Street
Minneapolis, Minn.

ANNA BERGELAND
Superintendent

DUpont 8341

Healthy normal Baby

May 11, 1949.

TO WHOM IT MAY CONCERN:

In looking up the record for Mrs. Mildred Johnsen age 23, 2024 North Girard, the patient entered the Deaconess Hospital December 21, 1937 at 8:50 p.m. and a baby boy was delivered at 8:20 A.M. December 23, 1937. Baby Boy Johnson, normal delivery L.O.A. position was admitted to the nursery- weight 5 pounds 15¾ oz.length 19½ inches. Identification Tape no.93, to mother and infant's wrist; Anklet "Johnson" clamped to baby's ankle. Baby and Mother discharged from the hospital December 31, 1937, Baby stayed 6 days; mother stayed 10 days, baby normal in every way. Mother discharged in good condition.
December 24,1937 blood from cord-Kline negative. Baby boy circumcised on December 30, 1937.

Daniel A. MacDonald, M.D.

K. G. NORBERG
5028 CHASE AVENUE
SKOKIE, ILLINOIS

June 24th, 1949

TO WHOM IT MAY CONCERN:

As nearly as I can remember it was in the late winter of 1948 that Mr. and Mrs. Bro Dahlberg called at our home in Minneapolis, Minn. and asked me to help them persuade Mr. and Mrs. Marvin Johnsen to let them take their little boy back and put him in a special school where they had had him before.

As I understood it the boy was not well and Mr. and Mrs. Dahlberg had arranged to get him in a school where he was receiving special care. He was getting along very well, but the parents took him out and brought him home to Minneapolis.

Mr. and Mrs. Dahlberg felt that this was very wrong to the child and insisted on that the parents put the boy back in this school again and they would assume all financial obligations.

As I questioned them regarding the motive back of it they assured me that they had no intention to try in any way to get the child away from them, which they feared the parents thought, but were only interested in the welfare of the boy and felt the parents were not in as good a position as they were to give the boy the attention that he needed.

In other words the interest that Mr. and Mrs. Dahlberg had was simply from a humanitarian stand point. They were vitally concerned about the boy's welfare and anxious to do every thing they could to help the parents give him the best of care and educational advantage.

K. G. Norberg

K. G. Norberg

STATE OF ILLINOIS)
) SS:
COUNTY OF COOK)

Subscribed and sworn to before me, a Notary Public, this 25th day of June A. D. 1949.

Wilbert Schuemann

Notary Public

Wilbert Schuemann, Notary Public
Cook County, Illinois
[illegible]

grandparents minister

K. G. NORBERG
5028 CHASE AVENUE
SKOKIE, ILLINOIS

June 24th, 1949

Mr. and Mrs. Marvin Johnsen
1515 Stoneman Avenue South
Alhambra, California.

My dear Mr. and Mrs. Johnson:

Your father called me today from Minneapolis and wanted to know if Mr. and Mrs. Bro Dahlberg said anything to me about adopting your little boy when they called on us in Minneapolis and wanted me to help them persuade you to let them take the boy and put him back in school again.

I told him no and that on the contrary when I questioned them why they were so anxious to get the boy, when you did not want to let him go, they assured me it was not that they wanted to get the boy away from you, but that they felt this school was doing so much for him since he was not well so it just broke their hearts to think you took him out, and were going to do every thing they could to get him back again. Dad asked me to put this in writing and have it notarized and send it to you at once. This I am doing for what it might be worth.

Very sincerely yours,

K G Norberg

P.S. Understand mother is with you. Please greet her from us.

K.G.N.

State of Minnesota
LUTHER W. YOUNGDAHL, GOVERNOR
Division of Social Welfare
117 UNIVERSITY AVENUE
St. Paul 1

JARLE LEIRFALLOM
DIRECTOR

L. MERRITT BROWN, CHIEF
CHILD WELFARE UNIT

June 27, 1949

Mr. Marvin Johnson,

1615 South Stoneman,

Alhambra, California

Dear Mr. Johnson,

At your request Mr. Edward Baran has inquired whether there is a Bror Dahlberg licensed boarding home or home for underprivileged children at International Falls.

Our records show no boarding home of this name and our Central Index has no registrations on the Bror Dahlberg family.

Very truly yours,

L. Merritt Brown, Chief,
Child Welfare Unit.

LMB/b

A REPORT TO PARENTS
MINNEAPOLIS PUBLIC SCHOOLS

THIS CARD BELONGS TO

Craig Johnson
PUPIL'S NAME

Douglas
NAME OF SCHOOL

DO NOT ROL

40 55M 5-46 Vocational School Print Shop

FINAL NOTE TO PARENTS

TEACHER'S COMMENTS:

Craig is doing
satisfactory work in
all his subjects. He
is well liked by the
class. He shows interest
in his work, and
works independently.

6 * Los Angeles Times
Part II—THURS., JUNE 16, 1949

Injunction Won by Dahlbergs in Custody Case

Superior Judge Clarence M Hanson yesterday issued a pr liminary injunction sought b Bror and Gilda Dahlberg to pre vent the parents of their 11-year old protege, Craig Marvin Johnsen, from removing him from a private school.

To serve "the best interests of the child," the judge stated, "the status quo should be preserved" pending trial of the custody suit. The boy is at the Chadwick School for Boys, placed there by the Dahlbergs.

Atty. Preston D. Orem, for Marvin and Mildred Johnsen, the parents, accused the wealthy industrialist and his wife of virtually attempting to buy the child.

Violation Claims

The Dahlbergs' charge which brought the injunction said the Johnsens had threatened to remove the boy to Minnesota, in violation of a 1948 penciled contract giving the wealthy pair the privilege of educating him to the age of 14. The youth's health is at stake, they claim.

The Johnsens, through Orem, denied they intended to take Craig out of the State but contended that the Dahlbergs had violated the contract themselves by refusing to permit them to exercise their visitation rights.

'Sale of A Child'

Orem argued that the contract itself was illegal in that it violated public policy, as "it relates to bargain and sale of a child for monetary consideration."

Consideration, he said, was transportation here from Minnesota for the Johnsen family, a job, a car and guarantee of $500 a month income, as well as medical care and schooling for Craig until he is 14, and $300 a month annuity for him after he reaches 18.

In the Dahlbergs' complaint, they claim they have spent $25,000 on the care and education of Craig during the past seven years, and $50,000 on the boy's family. Attorneys Buron Fitts and Hen-

STATEMENT OF: EDWARD S. BARAN, 2215 Blaisdell Ave So, Minneapolis, Minnesota.

I, Edward S. Baran, upon oath despose the following to be a true incident taken place in the city of Minneapolis, Minn sota, at the time Mr. Bror Dahlberg was in said city with Joseph Scott, Attorney at Law, practicing in Los Angeles, California on behalf of said Mr. Bror Dahlberg.

At the request of Mr. Milton Hultgren, brother of my wife, Mrs. Louise E. Baran, who was riding with me at the time, I picked up Mr. Milton Hultgren and Mr. Bror Dahlberg to allow them to use my automobile to go about their business while in said city. While driving to my home, in the automobile were Mr. Milton Hultgren, Mr. Bror Dahlberg, Mrs. Louise E. Baran, and myself enjoined in conversation regarding the matter at hand at that time, namely welfare of Craig Johnsen.

In the conversation, Mr. Bror Dahlberg stated that he could not see why Mr. Marvin Johnsen was such a heel for not taking the opportunities he was giving to him regarding a better position and greater future for himself with his plant in Los Angeles rather than the position of Mail Carrier with the Post Office Department of the United States, because he was talented and had good possibilities of making a success of the positâon offered.

Also, Mr. Bror Dahlberg was asked if hè planned to adopt Craig Johnseh because of all the hullabaloo made by his personal intervention in the matter, to which he definitely stated that under no circumstances would he ever permit his wife to take the child from its rightful parents. That would be as far as he would let his wife go with her actions, before he would put his foot down.

Edward S. Baran

Subscribed and sworn to this 27th day of June 1949,

Frank Oswald.

FRANK OSWALD,
Notary Public, Hennepin County, Minn.
My Commission Expires Sept. 6, 1951.

LAW OFFICES
PRESTON D. OREM

SUITE 806 NINTH AND HILL BUILDING
315 WEST NINTH STREET
LOS ANGELES 15
TRINITY 7451

November 29, 1951

C O P Y

Arvey, Hodes & Mantynband
Forty-Fourth Floor
One LaSalle Street
Chicago 2, Illinois

Attention: LeRoy R. Krein

Re: Johnsen vs. Dahlberg - 51 C 1439.

Dear Mr. Krein:

After receiving your letter of November 16, 1951, I had a conference with Mr. Marvin Johnsen. The Johnsens feel that before we are in a position to discuss any settlement of the alleged damages, that some arrangement should be made with respect to the past visitation rights.

Inasmuch as the Johnsens made the agreement with the Dahlbergs in absolute good faith, but shortly thereafter the Dahlbergs took the boy out of the state in direct violation of an order of our Superior Court, and have since kept the child out of the state, the Johnsen's feel Mr. Dahlberg should at least make some sort of arrangement whereby they can see their only son.

Will you kindly contact Mr. Dahlberg and ascertain his views upon this matter?

Yours very truly,

Signed Preston D. Orem
PRESTON D. OREM

AFFIDAVIT OF : MRS. GLADYS MADSEN, MINNEAPOLIS, MINNESOTA

I GLADYS MADSEN, upon oath despose the following to be true to the best of my knowledge:

One afternoon Elwin Madsen, my husband, "Doc Allen", and I were having lunch at the Nicollet Hotel, in Minneapolis, Minnesota prior to the time Mr. Marvin Johnsen accepted an offer from Mr. Bror Dahlberg for a position in Los Angeles, California. Some of the conversation concerned the matter of Mr. and Mrs. Marvin Johnsen and family's going to California regarding the position offered by Mr. Bror Dahlberg to Mr. Johnsen. I expressed my doubts to "Doc Allen", who was Mr. Bror Dahlberg's private masseur at that time, as to whether or not Mr. Marvin Johnsen would accept such a proposition to leave his work here due to the fact that Mrs. Gilda Dahlberg had on several occasions in the past never kept her word to the Johnsen family, and I could see no reason why she would keep her word on this offer of Mr. Bror Dahlberg's, made by him on Mrs. Gilda Dahlberg's behalf. To which "Doc Allen" replied in effect that Gilda Dahlberg would keep after this until she definitely had Craig Johnsen.

I further relate as to the character of the Mr. and Mrs. M. Johnsen and family, that I feel that one could find no finer a family for neighbors and friends. They were and are fine parents, taking very good care of their children while discharging their responsibilities as parents to their children as to schooling, cleanliness and health, and care of in a manner any community would be proud of. At most anytime one could find the children, also Craig any time he was home, enjoying the pleasures of childhood and playfulness of children in his home neighborhood indicative of a harmonious family and neighborhood life.

We, all the people in the neighborhood and friends of the Johnsen's at home and at work with Mr. Marvin Johnsen, regretted to see the Marvin Johnsen Family move to California, since they were and are so well liked by all that knew them and came in contact with them.

Mrs. Gladys Madsen

Mrs. Gladys Madsen, Minneapolis, Minn.

Subscribed and sworn to me this 27 day of June 1949,

Beatrice L. Johnson

MINNEAPOLIS PARENTS GET THEIR BOY BACK

Millionaire Loses Mailman's Son

SPECIAL TO MINNEAPOLIS TRIBUNE

G.M. HOLLYWOOD, CALIF. — Bror Dahlberg started to work for the Northern Pacific railroad in Minneapolis when he was 14, running a rope elevator.

He walked 11 miles each way to work. The family of six — Bror, his widowed mother and four other children—lived on the outskirts of the city, where rent was cheap.

Bror worked 12 hours a day and collected $15 a month. This taught him, he says now, that it didn't pay to be poor. He looked around for a way out. Today at 67 he is one of the country's richest men, chairman of the famous Celotex Corp., and guiding genius of a dozen other corporations.

HE CREDITS MOTHER

Bror attributes his success to his mother. (His father died shortly after the family came to this country from Sweden, when Bror was 11.) His mother told him when he was a small boy that you never get anything for nothing; that to succeed you have to give of yourself until there is nothing more to give.

Dahlberg seldom if ever has refused to give. Currently he's faced with bitter disappointment because one of his gifts has been rejected.

He has waged, and lost, an intense fight for the custody of 10-year-old Craig Johnsen, son of a Minneapolis mailman, who had been cared for by Dahlberg and his second wife for the last five years.

(1+2 years)

rubbed elbows with millionaires' sons.

The Dahlbergs became increasingly fond of Craig, and Bror offered to find the boy's father a job in California. The veteran mail carrier declined, doubting the job's stability.

Several reunions were arranged—Mrs. Johnsen was a guest at the Dahlberg home a (2) number of times, and the boy occasionally returned to Minnesota.

Things went along nicely until Bror recently filed a petition to legalize his guardianship of Craig.

As Dahlberg tells it, he had not planned to adopt the boy, but thought it wise to provide some legal basis for helping the lad in the future. Mrs. Johnsen had given her consent, he said. (WE)

BUT THINGS BLOW UP

He was more than somewhat surprised, therefore, when the mother descended in wrath on the Dahlberg home just before the Christmas holidays.

There were a series of heated talks. On Christmas day, Mrs. Johnsen says, things got even rougher and there were fisticuffs when Mrs. Dahlberg started to push her around.

At any rate, Mrs. Johnsen managed to get Craig out of the Dahlberg house.

Dahlberg got a restraining order that would have kept the boy in California pending a court decision, but he was a few hours too late. Mrs. Johnson already had left with Craig for Minneapolis.

STILL WANT HIM BACK

It seems unlikely the case will be carried any farther in the courts—but the Dahlbergs still would like to get the boy back.

Those who sympathize with Dahlberg believe he's only trying to spare Craig the troubles that Bror himself went through in his early life.

Bror's first job, as related, was running an elevator for the railroad. Then he bought a second-hand Pittman shorthand book for a nickel. That proved to be his key to success.

He taught himself shorthand and typing, and finally was efficient enough to get a stenographer's job. He worked his way up through various departments of the railroad and its lumbering

BROR DAHLBERG GILDA DAHLBERG CRAIG JOHNSEN MRS. JOHNSEN

Principals in the custody case millionaire Bror lost

Gilda slapped mother in the face so hard she had a red mark that lasted her lifetime.

NONE OF HIS OWN

Dahlberg, twice married, has no children of his own. That may also enter into his desire to raise Craig as his son.

The Dahlberg - Johnsen affair started some years back when Bror and his second wife, Gilda, met Mr. and Mrs. Marvin Johnsen of Minneapolis through a sister ← BROTHER of Mrs. Johnsen, a Dahlberg employe. (LIE)

CRAIG'S MARLYS
(5) (8)

The Johnsens were visiting at the Dahlberg summer place on Red Crest island, near Ranier, Minn., when Gilda Dahlberg became captivated by Craig, then a sickly child of 5. (LIE)

She asked the parents to let her take him to a Minneapolis doctor. The doctor reported, she says, that the child might not survive unless he was taken to a milder climate.

Gilda then persuaded Mr. and Mrs. Johnsen to let her take the frail boy to the Dahlberg home in California. (LIE)

← SHE TOOK HIM WITHOUT THEIR PERMISSION

LIVES LIKE PRINCE

There Craig responded to sunshine and the best care that money could buy. He was sent to an exclusive school, where he

business, and eventually went into the lumber business for himself.

That led to celotex.

LUMBER SUBSTITUTE

"I saw," he recalls, "that lumbering stood a good chance of running out in this country, and I began experimenting with something that would take its place."

In his experiments he came across bagasse, the stock of sugar cane after everything of value has been removed. In 1920 he set up his first mill near Orleans to manufacture celotex out of bagasse. Now he owns 16 mills over the world, including one in England and one in London.

When celotex clicked, Bror went into the sugar cane business, and now he owns cane plantations over the world.

From sugar he went into oil and into cemesto, a product he hopes will go a long way toward relieving the country's housing problem.

FIRST MARRIAGE FAILS

Along with his busy business life Dahlberg found time to marry twice, once not too happily.

His first wife was Mary Alexander, a social climber who, before she married Bror in 1921, had an extensive acquaintance with the elite of the Chicago underworld.

Bror and Mary were divorced in 1932, and in time Mary was to sue Bror for $40,000 in back alimony.

After a considerable airing of soiled linen, in which Bror claimed their marriage was never legal because Mary had been previously wed and never divorced, he settled out of court. The sum paid reportedly was $2,500.

HE AND GILDA GET ALONG

Bror married his present wife, Gilda, in May of 1932—less than a month after his divorce from Mary. Gilda, who is still pretty and unaffected, once was on the stage. Twenty years ago she played the lead in the Broadway musical, "Little Jessie James."

There's been scarcely a rumble

MINNEAPOLIS SUNDAY TRIBUNE
Jan. 18, 1948 1. ** 7

of discord in the 16 years Gilda and Bror have been married. She babies him and he seems to like it.

BOY BACK IN CITY

Paternity Expert in Custody Fight

JOSEPH SCOTT, attorney, stepped into the battle today between wives of a Minneapolis mailman and a California millionaire over custody of a 10-year-old boy.

Mrs. Bror Dahlberg, wife of the millionaire, former Twin Cities man, has hired Scott, according to Samuel Yorty, Los Angeles attorney for the mailman's wife, Mrs. Marvin Johnsen, 2315 Garfield avenue.

Scott represented Joan Barry in her successful paternity suit against Charlie Chaplin.

The boy, Craig, was back home in Minneapolis with his mother, Mrs. Johnsen, after she had used a ruse to get him away from the Dahlbergs, with whom he had been for the past three years.

Mrs. Johnsen allegedly was scratched by Mrs. Dahlberg in a dispute before she obtained possession of the boy, Yorty said. He added that he "may file suit against Mrs. Dahlberg for damages" on charges of assault and battery.

Scott

Scott was hired by Mrs. Dahlberg after she had dismissed another attorney, Yorty said.

A hearing on the Dahlbergs' petition for guardianship of the boy was scheduled for today in Los Angeles. It was expected to be laid over.

The Dahlbergs had obtained an order restraining Mrs. Johnsen from taking the boy out of California, but she already had left with him, Yorty added.

The youngster had been given over to the Dahlbergs' care three years ago by Mrs. Johnsen when the building materials manufacturer and his wife, now of Beverly Hills, Calif., were living in Minneapolis.

The alleged face-scratching episode occurred when Mrs. Johnsen went to California a few weeks ago to get the boy.

She finally gained his custody by taking him from the Dahlberg home, supposedly to go to church, but instead bringing him to the home of west coast relatives.

Mrs. Johnsen said today that she turned Craig over to the Dahlbergs because "he wasn't well—that was my only reason for letting him go."

"I'm not alarmed at anything," Mrs. Johnsen added. "I have papers to show they promised Craig back whenever I wanted him."

Mexico Trip – After 27 Years

About the Author:

Marlys (Johnsen) was born in Minneapolis Minnesota. She was married to Richard A. Norris of Roseboro, North Carolina on February 20, 1960 by the Rev. Henry Sundstrom of Pasadena, who had married her maternal grandparents nearly 50 years earlier. They have one daughter, Linda J.M. Baer and husband Roger of Palmdale, Ca. And Two wonderful grandsons, Trevor (13) and Kevin (8).

Early in the marriage they lived in Arcadia, Ca. and Marlys worked in the Personnel office of Sears Roebuck & Co. & a Receptionist/Secretary in the Temple City Chamber of Commerce in San Gabriel Valley before moving to Fair Oaks in Northern California in 1990.

Writing has been a hobby of Marlys' for several years and her work published in both Southern and Northern California Newspapers.

She is a member of the Sacramento Suburban Writers and Sacramento Christian Writers and Sonrise Christian Groups.

She and Joe Baginski, Counselor are Coauthoring a book titled "Recipes for a Happier Marriage."

Printed in the United States
21799LVS00004B/200